Balcony Gardening

Growing Herbs and Vegetables in a Small Urban Space

Jeff Haase

Published by Balcony Books

To Katie and Justin
my little garden helpers

First Edition,
Published in 2013 by Balcony Books
Toronto, Canada

ISBN 978-0-9879732-0-7

www.mybalconyjungle.com

Contents

Introduction

I've grown lots of things on my little balcony: small trees, berries, lilies, shade-loving perennials and lots of garden center annuals. But I get the most pleasure out of growing herbs and vegetables. My initial motivation to grow something was to provide shade. I wanted to be able to sit on my balcony and be surrounded by plant life. I wasn't too particular about what I was growing so long as it was big and bushy. And growing a crowded mess of large plants became my goal. I loved walking through my neighbourhood and looking up at my building to see all that vegetation way up on my balcony. And with the plants arranged just right, I could sit out there and be completely shaded from the sun and feel just a little cut off from the city around me.

Several years ago my wife and I were shopping at a farmers market, admiring some plump heirloom tomatoes and sweet mini watermelons. We thought it would be nice to own a home close to a farmers market so we could just pop over and buy great produce whenever we wanted. But it occurred to me that even with my limited gardening experience it shouldn't be too difficult to grow fat juicy heirloom tomatoes myself, right on our balcony. And how hard could it really be to grow a watermelon?

My balcony is on the 18th floor of a condo high-rise in the suburbs of Toronto, Canada. It faces west but is also open to the north. During the summer months, direct sunlight starts to strike the balcony from around 1 PM until sunset. The half walls around the outside of the balcony are solid and prevent all but an hour or two of sunlight from reaching pots on the balcony floor close to the half wall. It can get windy but it's not that bad. Usually in late spring and early summer we spend time on the balcony but we find late afternoons in the middle of July to be a little too hot.

I don't give much consideration to how my garden looks. I don't mind the plastic containers and clutter. I place my plants based on their needs: not mine. I don't consider myself to be a master gardener. I don't have time to truly become an expert and besides, there is always something new to learn. My goals are simple: to grow food in a space that wouldn't otherwise be used. I'm not looking to grow record breaking vegetables or achieve bumper yields. I just want to grow stuff.

Small space container gardening is not rocket science. Patience and knowledge go a long way. Get to know the limits of your space and set your expectations accordingly. You will not be self-sufficient growing container vegetables on a typical city balcony. But you should easily be able to grow a nice selection of fresh herbs and juicy tomatoes. This is a book for beginner gardeners and those wondering if it's possible to do anything on their balcony other than sip coffee, watch traffic zoom by, store a bicycle or hang laundry. Although it's titled "Balcony Gardening", you could easily apply the information in this book to container gardening on a terrace, a fire escape, a rooftop garden… pretty much anywhere you can imagine.

It takes a lot of sunshine to grow most vegetables and even those that can tolerate a bit of shade will not grow well if at all with lots of it. If your balcony is deeply shaded and you have a desire to grow herbs and vegetables you will need to seek out an alternative growing space. Find a plot in a community garden. Convince your landlord or condo board to let you garden a patch of the yard. Or find a friend or relative open to the idea of you setting up a small garden on their property in exchange for some of your harvest. Cities are full of little patches of under-utilized land just waiting to be cultivated!

The Challenges of Balcony Gardening

To be a successful balcony gardener you need to overcome several challenges that make growing on a balcony different from growing on the ground. Some obvious things are lack of space and no actual soil to garden in. But these are just constraints you can easily work around. There are other environmental obstacles and barriers that make balcony gardening a challenge. A balcony can be a very hostile environment for container bound plants. And all balconies are not created equal. What works on one will not necessarily work on another.

Sunlight

Even in the deepest outdoor shade you can grow some very beautiful and interesting plants. But not vegetables. You can get by with a bit of shade for some vegetable crops but you really need full sun to grow vegetable plants that thrive. Here's how I like to categorize sunlight conditions.

☼   Full Sun means unobstructed access to direct sunlight for more than 6 hour a day

☼   Partial Shade or Partial Sun means 3 to 6 hours of direct sunlight per day with partial sun being at the top of the range and partial shade, the bottom. Partial shade may also be achieved with dappled sunlight: a spotty sunlight pattern such as that projected through the leaves of another plant.

✸   Full Shade implies less than a few hours of direct sunlight per day

The orientation of your building and location of your balcony as well as the shadows cast by surrounding walls, railings and overhangs, will affect the amount of direct sunlight your balcony receives. Obviously, a balcony that is set back into the building will be more sunlight challenged and if you have an overhang over your balcony (like mine) you will miss out on a large part of the day's sunshine. This is something roof top gardeners never have to worry about.

You may need to consider changes in the sun's elevation during the season. Watch the lighting patterns on your balcony to see what areas receive the most light and how it changes from month to month. Don't assume that just because your balcony faces south you will be blessed with endless rays of sunlight.

Even the colour of the walls around your balcony will affect the amount of indirect sunlight your plants receive as dark colours absorb light and bright colours reflect it. Brightly painted walls and floors will reflect a small amount of light back towards your plants.

Some modern balconies have glass half walls around their edges and these are ideal for letting sunlight through. A metal or wood railing will let lots of light onto your balcony as well and can also serve as a convenient place for climbing plants to anchor onto. My balcony has a solid half wall around it that lets no light through. It casts a huge shadow on all plants set on the floor of the balcony for most of the day.

Fruit bearing plants and many herbs will require as much sunlight as you can provide. Some will be somewhat productive in partial sun but the closer to shady conditions they get, the less productive they will be. Some plants will not grow as strong and will most likely fail to flower or ripen fruit without proper sunlight. I've grown pepper plants that refused to flower in partial shade but exploded with tiny peppers once I moved them over just a few feet to a sunnier spot on my balcony.

Water

If your garden is open to the sky above then you might enjoy a free watering from the rain every now and then. But don't count on it being enough to keep your plants constantly watered and happy. Container bound plants dry out fast. Grown in the ground, a plant can extend its roots over a wide area and deep into the soil in search of moisture. Container soils lose moisture to increased evaporation thanks to the wind and sun. And the extra heat and wind the plants experience on a balcony make them use what little water they have in their containers much faster.

If you don't have an outdoor faucet available to connect a garden hose, all of your water will have to be carried in a watering can or bucket from the kitchen sink to the balcony. I always underestimate how long it takes every morning to water my plants. During the dog days of summer I use well over 10 gallons of water to keep my balcony plants hydrated. And some plants I end up having to water twice a day.

Wind

High rise balconies and roof tops are windy places. Wind tends to blow faster and harder the higher above the ground you go. Wind also gets funneled around objects it encounters, like your building, causing it to compress and flow more forcefully around the edges. And as the wind slams up against flat surfaces it will bounce and deflect, changing direction and causing turbulent and unpredictable micro blasts of air.

A windy day on my balcony, which faces west, usually means plants up against the back wall get thrashed about the worst so I like to move them out to the outer edge of the balcony. But they still get whipped around by the wind that gets redirected off the building and flows back along the floor towards the outer wall. The plants placed there tend to experience interesting updrafts. It takes a bit of observation to know how every square foot of your growing space will be affected by the wind and what will grow best in all places.

Strong winds can give your balcony plants quite a beating. Especially during hot sunny days when the summer heat wilts the leaves making them less resistant to damage. But a good amount of air flow is also required for healthy plant growth. The wind will cause the plants to transpire more, making them draw more moisture and nutrients from the potting soil. Some plants need a breeze to assist with pollination. And a good breeze also helps to strengthen your plants so they can support additional plant mass and fruit load.

To reduce wind exposure, you may be able to construct a wall or fence that is anchored to the building. Do not under estimate the damage a good wind gust can do. Any temporary or otherwise movable screen you put up to block the wind that is not properly anchored down, will get blown over. If you do erect some kind of screen be sure it is secure (very secure) and that having it on the balcony does not break any of your building rules. Anchoring the screen to a wall or the floor may not go over too well with your landlord or property manager. And the last thing you want is something similar to a large sheet of plywood blowing off your balcony and sailing into unsuspecting traffic below.

I've seen balconies where the wind was just too great for anything to grow. One possible solution is a portable greenhouse. These can be purchased from hardware stores and garden centers and typically consist of a metal stand with a heavy clear plastic cover placed over it. This will keep the wind out and keep the warm air and moisture in.

Bugs and Critters

The nice thing about being high up on a balcony is that you rarely have to deal with animals invading your garden. No mice, no deer, and for many of us, no cats, rabbits or raccoons either. Oddly enough though, even on the 18th floor, I have seen squirrels. Pigeons used to be a problem for me until I had some pigeon netting installed and for a while it made the balcony feel like an extension of our indoor living space.

But this disconnection with nature also has its drawbacks. Fewer insects make their way up this high. I see a few bees and the occasional ladybug. But it pales in comparison to what visits a land-based garden. I do not get enough insects to reliably pollinate melons or squash. I also do not benefit from the activity of insects living beneath my soil surface, like worms and beetles that dig and plow through the soil, loosening it and transporting nutrients.

Other invaders do occasionally make their way onto the balcony. Aphids, spider mites and whiteflies can easily hitch a ride on new plants introduced to your balcony. And once these invaders establish themselves they will likely remain season after season unless you personally do something about them. These pest insects have natural predators that normally keep them in check but it is unlikely you'll be seeing many of those on your balcony.

Weight

How much weight can your balcony carry? You will likely never find a definitive answer. The balconies of modern high-rise buildings, with reinforced poured concrete construction, should be able to handle an extensive container garden. But it's the fire escapes, rooftop terraces and wooden decks on older buildings that I have the most concern for. I've always believed that if it is safe for me and my family to stand around on our balcony, what is it going to matter if I have a few potted plants out there also. But you should at least have an appreciation for how much your potted plants weigh before you consider dismissing weight as a non issue.

To give you an idea, here are a couple of examples from my balcony. A typical plant for me is a large 6 foot tomato plant growing in a 5 gallon bucket. During the peak of my growing season, this plant, container and all, will weight over 30 lbs after being watered. My larger self-watering container in which I usually grow a pair of larger tomato plants can weigh over 110 lbs with a full water reservoir. I have three containers similar to this one and sometimes as many as 7 large single containers out there at the same time. Combined, when watered, these containers can weigh as much 540 lbs.

Building Rules and Neighbours

If you live in a condo or apartment building there may be rules in place that limit what you can put on your balcony. These rules typically exist to keep residents from doing things on their balcony that might pose a risk to others, lower property values or just annoy their neighbours. It would be a shame to put lots of effort into raising a small fruit tree only to have to get rid of it because it violates some building by-law. Check your building rules to see what you can and cannot have on your balcony before investing in big containers and potting soil. Don't be surprised if all you can put out there is basic outdoor furniture and a few plants. You may have a restriction that says nothing can be visible above the outside railings.

What you may perceive to be a beautiful thing might not be seen that way by others. In a condominium, property values are affected by the appearance of the building and if your garden is untamed and wild, some may see it as a distraction that takes away form the value of the property. Especially in the fall when everything starts to die off and you've been neglecting your pruning.

Another classic source of neighbourly tension is container run-off, dripping from your balcony to those below. You will probably notice that few of your neighbours use their balconies for anything other than storage. But some do maintain tidy balconies and if you have nothing set up to catch the run-off from your containers during watering you could be faced with an upset neighbour who doesn't appreciate water dripping onto their balcony from above.

Planning your Garden

Many gardeners, myself included, spend the winter thinking about what to plant next season and when spring comes, we waste no time getting down to business. But as the summer rolls in and vacation plans take shape, the garden gets neglected. That early springtime ambition fades fast. Plants go un-watered and grow over-crowded, untamed and unloved.

Planning a productive vegetable garden for a small urban space can present some challenges. There is literally less room for error in a balcony garden. You have to learn to limit yourself to what you can realistically grow given the limitations of your balcony. Prepare for the season and do your research.

Too crowded! Many of the plants pictured here were not receiving enough sunlight

What To Plant

I have grown some plants and wondered later what I was thinking. The seed catalogs always come early. And some of the bigger catalogs I receive are always full of glossy images showing overflowing baskets of perfect vegetables with descriptions promising early and bountiful harvests. When these catalogs come out during the depths of winter it's hard to apply restraint.

The best plants to grow are the ones you know you will enjoy. It sounds simple enough but sometimes it's hard not to be persuaded by something interesting or exotic in a seed catalog or garden center. Personally, I get more out of gardening when I've grown something my family will actually eat. But you should also keep some room to try something new and experiment a little from time to time.

You should also figure out the length of your growing season and restrict yourself to plants that will have time to grow and mature within your growing time frame. Some plants need a long hot growing season and you want to ensure they have plenty of time to produce fruit that will ripen. In some cases, starting plants early and indoors will be necessary.

Make It All Fit

It is very easy to crowd a balcony garden. I don't know how many times I've started out with more than I've had space to grow. It all fits nicely at the beginning of the season when the plants are small and tidy. But as the season wears on and the plants stretch out and spread, you can quickly find yourself overwhelmed. And more plants do not necessarily lead to more vegetables. Over planting a small space can create a lot of shade. The plants all compete for limited sunlight and when crowded together, none of them win. Fortunately it only takes 5 minutes and a good set of pruners to remedy a crowded balcony.

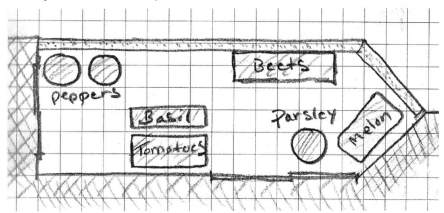

A simple little sketch can help in a big way

If you want to maximize the use of your space but can't seem to visualize how it's all going to fit, sketch it out. Measure your balcony and draw a scale floor plan. Or just a rough sketch will do. Know where the sunny spots in your space are and figure out where things should go. Allow for the spread of the plants when they are mature and don't forget to also consider their height.

Gather Up What You Need

Most seed companies have pretty good turn around times but smaller companies may take a while to process your order. And everyone else is likely buying seed from them at the same time you are. Don't wait until the last minute to purchase seed from seed vendors.

It doesn't take much effort to start a few extra plants in case you encounter setbacks. If you want to grow a single watermelon plant from seed, start three or four. You can even put them all out in the spring to harden off. But resist the urge to plant the extras. If you have space for one, just grow one. Trust me. Compost the extras or give them to a friend.

Garden centers and nurseries sell lots of new vegetable and herb plants in the spring but they won't be there forever. Resist the urge to purchase them too early unless you know you can give them a proper early start. But don't wait too long either because once they sell out, you won't see them again until next spring.

Follow a Plan

Plan ahead and watch the calendar. Know how long each plant you plan to start from seed takes to germinate and grow to transplant size. Have a good idea when the weather outside will be warm enough to start planting. Cucumbers and melons don't like cool weather or soil. But if started indoors you don't want them to get too big in their starter pots either. Fruiting plants like tomatoes and peppers only set fruit when the temperature is within a specific range so those plants need to reach a mature size before those temperatures arrive. You may even need to bring plants indoors or cover them to protect them from a late frost or unusually cool spring night.

Consider staggering crops and make use of successive plantings to keep your containers actively producing for you throughout the season. With a bit of upfront planning you can have a continuous harvest, even from a single container.

Keep a journal or blog of what you grow, when you plant, where you obtained seedlings, when you harvested, what type of fertilizers you used, how much and how often. All of these notes will be useful when you need to plan out your garden for next season.

Gardening Tools and Other Useful Items

There are many useful and not so useful gardening tools available. And there are only a few that I find really necessary for a small-scale container garden. This is my assortment of garden tools and other useful things that I've been using on the balcony for some time now.

Watering Can

Even if you have an outdoor faucet and hose, you may still want to use a watering can for watering container plants. Just about anything that can hold water will do. Preferably something with a handle. I've been using the same old 2 gallon plastic watering jug for years. A bigger can means less trips to the sink but it also means more weight to carry. Make sure your watering can has a detachable spray head so you can remove it when you just need to get water someplace in a hurry. Use the spray head when watering the soil directly to avoid soil compaction and seed displacement. I lost the spray head for my favorite watering can a long time ago and I really should find another one.

Small Trowel

Next to a watering can, this is the one tool I use most often. It helps to have one with a sharp point that can dig into root bound containers. The one small plastic shovel I have has served me well for several years. I've also been known to use a spoon or chopstick from the kitchen for working with seeds and seedlings.

Pruners

For the longest time I used to do my pruning with a big pair of scissors and I don't know how I used to manage it. A good set of pruning shears will make quick work of even the toughest plant. They are great for keeping tomato plants under control but what I use them for most is pruning everything down at the end of the season. This is by far the most expensive gardening tool I own.

Spray Bottle

I keep a pair of these on the balcony. One I keep filled with water and use it to mist down the soil in newly planted seed and seedling containers to keep them moist. The other I keep topped up with a mild soapy solution and a bit of neem oil, loaded and ready to beat back spider mites and mildew. I think I paid $1 for one of them and the other was free.

Neem oil is oil that has been pressed from the fruit and seeds of the neem tree. It is an organic insecticide and fungicide that is supposedly non-toxic to humans. I originally tried using it to get rid of aphids but found in my case it wasn't very effective. But it does work well against mildew and spider mites so I continue to use small doses of it in my spray bottle. It is a bit expensive but a small amount can go a long way.

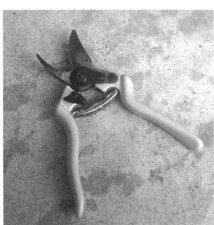 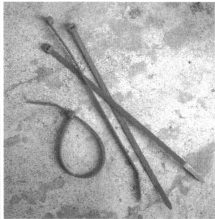

Bypass pruners and cable ties. Two of my favorite balcony gardening tools.

Those four items are what I consider "need to have" tools on my balcony. Here are some other useful items I like to keep around:

Bamboo poles

I have a good collection of sticks ranging from 2 to 6 feet in length. Bamboo is strong and flexible making it great for providing support. They are fairly easy to come by in my area but they are not cheap. Fortunately these poles are reusable and I don't need too many.

Cable Ties

I used to tie everything up with string and twine before I realized I had a fairly large supply of plastic cable ties in my storage room. I use them for tying poles together to make temporary ad-hoc trellises. Sometimes when I'm feeling lazy I use them to secure stems and branches to support poles but doing this does have a tendency to damage the plant. You have to be careful not to tighten them too much around the plant stems. They are very convenient and strong but not reusable.

Extra Storage Tote

I don't have yard space onto which I can dump out containers of used potting soil. So I like to keep an empty storage tote available for mixing potting soils and emptying containers for whatever reason.

Small Rake

I'm not sure where mine came from but I use it to mix up potting soils and turn compost. It is something I thought I could easily live without but it is actually quite useful.

Large Shovel

I have a large square shovel on my balcony that comes in handy for mixing batches of potting soil or cleaning up. I could get by without it and it's not something I bought for the balcony anyhow. It just ended up out there and occasionally makes itself useful.

Min-Max Thermometer

I keep a digital wireless thermometer inside that has a battery-powered sensor outside on the balcony to track outdoor temperatures. The thermometer keeps track of the highest and lowest temperatures until cleared. An outdoor min-max thermometer like this can help you track daily temperature highs and lows to determine the best time to start planting.

Containers

The most important thing to consider when choosing containers for your balcony garden is drainage. Make sure your containers have an adequate number of exit holes in the bottom for excess water to drain away. Overly moist soil will limit the oxygen available to a plant's roots, potentially suffocating them. Containers without enough drain holes should have more cut into them if possible. You can never have too many.

For me, weight is another important consideration. I'm not overly concerned about the weight load on my balcony but I like to have the freedom to reposition my plants and sometimes take them inside when the weather turns foul. Heavy containers make this more troublesome.

Containers that are tapered, large at the top and small at the bottom, are very common. But you get more space for roots with something cylindrical or cubic in shape; the same size at the top and bottom. And containers with a wider bottom are more stable and less likely to topple over in a strong wind.

Know what you're planting and how much spread and depth each plant will require below the soil surface. It is important to choose a container large enough to accommodate a plant's ever growing roots system. Plants with roots that completely fill their container are said to be root bound. There is no space for new root growth and when this happens the plant will stop growing. But at the same time, you don't want to choose containers that are unnecessarily large when your space is limited.

Here are some different container types to consider using on your balcony:

Clay Terracotta

> Terracotta containers are cheap and readily available and if they aren't colourful enough for you, you can always paint them. But they are heavy and I find the larger clay containers to be much too heavy for use on my balcony. Unglazed clay ceramics are porous and they will absorb moisture and draw it out of your potting soil. Plants in these containers will dry out quicker which can be good for plants that prefer a drier growing environment. These containers also have a tendency to crack when left outside during a cold frosty winter. The few terracotta containers I have had on the balcony all eventually got dropped or bumped and crack or shatter beyond use. Because they are porous, salts that accumulate inside these containers will eventually leach through the clay wall to the outside and this can appear unsightly.

Glazed Ceramic

I sometimes buy smaller decorative ceramic containers for smaller plants. Glazed ceramic containers are not porous like their unglazed counterparts so they will not draw moisture out of your potting soil. But they are just as heavy. I once had a glazed strawberry container I left on the balcony over the winter and in the spring all the glaze had cracked off. Some of the smaller glazed pots I own have matching ceramic trays glued to the bottom to catch run-off. These containers are great for small herbs. Especially those you plan to keep indoors through the winter.

Plastic

Plastic containers are my balcony gardening container of choice. They are lightweight and keep the moisture in the soil. But it does get hot fast when exposed to the sun which can quickly overheat a plant's roots. Some plastic containers, particularly those not intended for gardening use, will deteriorate and break apart over time when exposed to sunlight. Plastic containers are not all that attractive although you can purchase a wide assortment of shapes and sizes in a few different colours and they can be painted. I prefer plastic because it is affordable and it weighs next to nothing. Don't have drainage holes? No problem. Unlike ceramic it is very easy to drill and cut through plastic.

Wood

Wood planters look great and if treated properly, can last a number of seasons. For outdoor use, in terms of price and durability, the best wood to use is cedar. Redwood, cypress and teak also stand up to the elements but cost considerably more than cedar. Although wood containers look nice they can be heavy and take up considerable space. To extend their life, line them with heavy plastic or use an inner plastic container to hold potting soil. If you're handy and up to the challenge it shouldn't take too much imagination or effort to design and build your own custom wood planter. Avoid using pressure-treated lumber for planter construction projects. The chemicals used to preserve this sort of lumber can be toxic and will leach into potting soils.

Pretty much any container with the right dimensions can be used for growing vegetables if it has proper drainage. Almost any kind of bucket or tub will do. You can even grow plants like tomatoes and potatoes right in a bag of soil. No container necessary.

Potting Soil

Although we call it soil, it really is not. For your plants to grow strong and healthy in a container, the growing media must be resistant to compaction and have high moisture retaining qualities. It should be made up of materials that provide and maintain voids in the soil structure for roots to grow into and at the same time absorb moisture and nutrients like a sponge and release them slowly over time. Garden soils, straight from a bag or the ground, just aren't good enough on their own for growing plants in containers.

Why You Should Not Use Garden Soils

The roots of a plant need oxygen to survive. Air reaches the roots through small voids in the soil. Take away these voids and the plant will not be able to receive oxygen at its roots. With every watering, the soil particles in the container compact, making it harder for water to drain away and oxygen to penetrate. Without these voids, new roots can not form, existing root structure dies and your plant stops growing.

This is why garden soils, like top soil, are terrible for container gardening unless they contain additional materials to keep them loose. The fine particles in these "real" soils compact far too easily when used on their own in containers. On the ground, in gardens, worms and insects burrow around in the soil, loosening it up. This is not typically the case in a container on your balcony. What works great in a garden or flower bed will cause headaches for the container gardener – trust me.

Potting Soil Components

When you pick up a bag of potting soil at a garden center, these are some of the things you will usually find inside:

Peat Moss

> Peat moss has amazing water retention qualities. The peat moss we use in North America is partially decayed sphagnum moss that formed in Canadian bogs, marshes and wetlands. It is fibrous and very light with a nice spongy quality. It also raises the acidity levels of soils to which it is added (which is sometimes a good thing). Gardeners use it to lighten their soils and it is the most common and abundant component in potting soils. Over time, the peat in your potting soil will break down and make available a small (perhaps insignificant) amount of nitrogen.

Perlite

Vermiculite

Perlite

Perlite, which is an expanded form of volcanic glass, is incredibly light and porous making it great for preventing soil compaction and increasing water retention. It does not compress and retains its shape over time. Because it is so light, when mixing this into a potting soil on its own, be sure there isn't a strong breeze blowing when you pour it out of the bag or it will blow away.

Vermiculite

Vermiculite is a mineral similar to perlite in that it starts out as a naturally occurring mineral that is heated so that it expands to form a light spongy material that has great water retention properties. It has a worm or accordion like shape to it. Because it absorbs water and nutrients like a sponge and releases them slowly over time it makes an excellent soil amendment. Eventually it will break down in your potting soil, appearing as small shiny golden flakes.

Humus

Humus is the end product of the composting process and you may see the terms compost and humus used interchangeably. However compost is decaying organic matter whereas humus will not break down further. It has great water retention properties, contains many trace elements and minerals that plants require and provides an ideal living environment for beneficial microorganisms.

Fertilizers

Fertilizer is plant food. It contains nutrients that plants need to grow. Inorganic potting soils may contain a slow-release inorganic fertilizer but organic potting soils will almost always contain compost which is the most effective natural way to provide a balance of nutrients that your plants need to grow. Regardless of what sort of fertilizer your store bought potting soil starts out with, it will not be anywhere near enough to support your vegetable plants through the entire growing season.

Sand

Sand is sometimes used in container soils to assist with drainage. The sand does not absorb water so containers with sand in their potting soil will drain more readily. For most container-grown vegetables, you shouldn't need a potting soil that has much if any sand in it.

Other things you might find in commercially available potting soils are chemicals and minerals to balance the pH (page 21), beneficial fungi to assist roots with nutrient uptake and polymer gel crystals that assist with water retention.

What To Look For In A Potting Soil

Different plants have different needs. Some plants need better drainage than others. And some actually prefer to be grown in soils low in nutrients. Even so, my advice is to keep things simple and pick an all around well balanced potting soil mix and use it with everything. You can purchase potting soil ingredients separately to create your own potting soil, allowing you to mix and match composts and fertilizers of your choice. To be honest though, for the amount of potting soil I go through and the space limitations I have, I find it better to just buy bags of quality potting soil and add a little extra compost, perlite and vermiculite to them.

When purchasing potting soil, always read the label on the bag and understand exactly what it is you are buying. All potting soils are not created equal. You can really see the difference in the cheaper mixes which will be mostly peat moss and very little of anything else. Other less welcome and undocumented "things" you are likely to find, particularly in the cheaper potting soils, are sticks, stones and big chunks of tree bark. A good bag of potting soil, especially one used for starting seedlings, should be free of these unwanted materials.

Recycling Your Potting Soil

You do not need to restart each season with new potting soil. There is nothing wrong with reusing some of your potting soil from the previous season. Each year in the spring I uproot last year's dead plants and shake out the old root balls into a large plastic storage bin. To this I add new compost, some vermiculite and/or perlite to lighten it up.

Peat breaks down over time and your plants will consume some of the organic material in the potting soil during the growing season. And no matter how hard you shake them, you won't be able to free all of the potting soil trapped in those old root balls. But you probably don't want to keep it all anyways. Replacing a good percentage of the potting soil helps to reduce the concentration of mineral salts that will have built up over the previous season and the addition of new potting soil will also help maintain an acceptable soil pH level. On average I reclaim half of my potting soil from the previous season which means I'll still need to buy more to start again in the spring.

When you reuse a potting soil there is always a risk that any diseases, spores or bugs left behind will come back to haunt you next season. I have heard of people baking their old potting soil to sterilize it, to kill off bad spores and such. But I really can't see how anyone can be bothered to do this. An alternative to reusing it is to turn out all of your old potting soil into a garden or composter and start fresh every season with new bags of soil. But this can be rather expensive.

A very dense tomato plant root ball

It can take thousands of years for peat moss to form so I find it difficult to justify calling peat a renewable resource. Harvesting peat requires the stripping and drainage of wetland ecosystems. A good alternative to peat is coir: the fiber extracted from coconut husks. But with peat being so readily available it will likely be a long time before anything comes along to completely replace it.

Mineral Salts in Potting Soil

Salt accumulation will appear as a whitish substance caking on the surface of your container soil or around the inside rims of your containers. Mineral salts from tap water and inorganic fertilizers remain in the soil after the water carrying them has been removed through evaporation or transpiration Over time these salts build up enough to be visibly noticeable. My tap water is pH neutral and not too soft or too hard. To get it that way my municipality likely adds a number of salts and minerals to the water during treatment. These salts that remain behind in the potting soil affect its chemistry and will alter its pH. Plants have a hard time drawing moisture from soils that are saturated with mineral salts.

To remove some of the unwanted salt buildup from the potting soil in your containers you can flush them. Flushing your containers means pouring a considerable amount of water into them: at least as much water as the volume of the container you are flushing. Self-watering containers will also suffer from excess salt accumulations and they too may benefit from a good flushing from time to time, if you can manage it. I do this occasionally with my indoor houseplants by placing them in the kitchen sink and watering them repeatedly as water flows freely out the container drain holes. But on the balcony with large plants in heavy containers, this isn't going to be practical. Especially if the run-off from your containers is going to flow onto a neighbours balcony. Doing this will also flush lots of the nutrients out of the soil. For these reasons I have never bothered to flush my outdoor containers.

Soil pH

A container gardener who routinely replaces large quantities of potting soil at the start of each season should never have to worry about soil pH.

pH is the measure of how acidic or basic a solution is. It is represented on a scale that ranges from 0 to 14 with 7 being neutral. Anything below 7 is considered acidic and anything above 7 is said to be basic or alkaline. For example, vinegar, being very acidic, will have a pH of 2. Soapy water, being full of soap which is very basic, will have a pH up around 12. Good municipal tap water will have a pH of 7.

Plants are happy when the water they drink is within their preferred pH range and for most plants, a pH of 6.5 is perfect. The availability of nutrients varies with pH, particularly some of the micro nutrients. They become less available as the pH rises above neutral. When the pH levels of water in the potting soil become too acidic or basic, plants can have trouble acquiring the nutrients they require, even if the nutrients have been added to the soil in abundance.

Your potting soil will act as a buffer, shifting the pH of the water you add to it towards its pH. Soils from different regions have different pH buffering abilities and the same goes for potting soils. It's usually a safe bet that a good quality potting soil mix designed for growing vegetables will have its pH chemically adjusted to a comfortable 6.5.

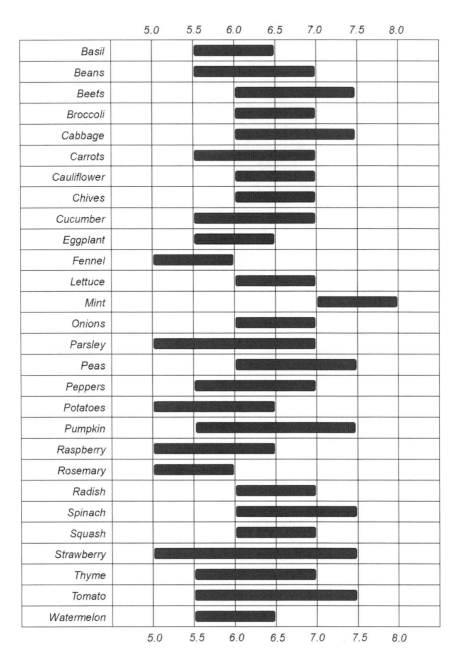

Preferred soil pH ranges for different herbs and vegetables

Testing for pH

If you're curious to learn a little more about your potting soil chemistry, you can always splurge on a pH test kit and measure the pH for yourself. When it comes to testing pH, you get what you pay for. Accuracy tends to vary directly with the cost of the test. The simplest and cheapest of pH test kits are chemical tests that consist of a vial for holding water and an additive that will cause the water mixed with soil in the vial to change colour depending on its pH. By comparing the colour of the test sample to a chart that comes with the test kit, you can get a rough idea of the sample pH level.

I find the best way to perform a test like this is to water the plant thoroughly so water runs out the bottom of the container. Collect this run-off and use it as a sample.

Another method for testing soil pH is with a pH meter. There are some really good (and expensive) professional meters available but there are also several inexpensive meters that can do the job. But generally you pay more for accuracy. The cheaper devices are nothing more than a pair of long metal probes that can be inserted into a muddy soil sample with a small meter at the top of the device indicates pH.

Changing the pH

The traditional way to raise soil pH is with the use of lime and you can lower the pH with sulfur. But adding these ingredients to older potting soils may not always be effective. Over time, the buffering capacity of your potting soil will degrade and it will no longer remain at 6.5, no matter what you add to it. Eventually there comes a time when you just have to replace it to make things right again.

If the pH has drifted over time due to the addition of salts to the soil during watering, occasionally flushing your containers to leach some of these salts from the soil will help to keep the pH balanced.

Be careful when attempting to adjust the pH of your potting soil. If you feel you must use an additive then do so in small amounts and give the additive plenty of time (weeks perhaps) to react with the soil and take effect. And keep in mind that your pH measurements may not be very accurate to begin with. A sudden and/or significant change to the chemistry of a potting soil can quickly kill the plants living in it.

Nutrients

Nutrients are things that all plants need to grow. With the exception of carbon, hydrogen and oxygen which plants get from water and the atmosphere, all of the mineral nutrients plants need will come from the soil in which they are planted. As plants die and rot, the nutrients locked within them are returned to the soil where they can be used by new plants. Obviously that's not going to happen much in your container garden, so you will need to add fertilizers to your potting soil to provide the necessary nutrients your plants need to grow.

NPK and more

The three most important mineral nutrients are the primary macronutrients: nitrogen, phosphorous and potassium.

Nitrogen (N)

> Nitrogen is considered to be the most important of the macro nutrients. Simply put, it is used by plants to create more plant matter.

Phosphorous (P)

> Phosphorous is necessary for flower formation, fruit set and root growth. It is also required for photosynthesis. It is a main component in the production of plant cell DNA.

Potassium (K)

> Potassium helps regulate plant growth. It assists with transpiration which allows a plant to transport water and nutrients up from the soil. Potassium makes plants strong and promotes disease resistance.

These three together provide the bulk of what a growing plant needs. When you purchase fertilizers you will find the percent concentration of these nutrients given by what is known as NPK. This is the percentage by weight of each of the primary macronutrients in that particular fertilizer. A fertilizer with an NPK of 10-7-3 will contain 10% nitrogen, 7% phosphorous and 3% potassium.

There are other secondary macronutrients, not as popular but just as important, required in smaller amounts by growing plants. They are calcium (Ca), chlorine (Cl), magnesium (Mg) and sulfur (S). Silicon (Si) is sometimes included in this group as well.

And finally there are a whole bunch of lesser nutrients known as micronutrients or trace elements. These are required in very small amounts:

boron (B), copper (Cu), iron (Fe), manganese (Mn), molybdenum (Mo) and zinc (Zn).

Store-bought potting soils will contain something that will provide some of the basic nutrients your plants need. Perhaps an inorganic slow-release additive or a small amount of compost. Whatever it is, it will not be enough to keep vegetable plants growing through a full season.

Organic versus Inorganic

Inorganic or synthetic fertilizers are easy to come by in garden centers. Although they contain fairly high concentrations of the primary macronutrients they typical contain very few of the other nutrients. These fertilizers are produced from non-renewable resources. Potassium and phosphorous are mined and synthetic nitrogen is made using industrial processes that consume large amounts of energy.

These synthetic fertilizers can provide your plants with readily available nutrients almost instantly as they are water soluble and do not have to break down in the soil to be available. For this reason you have to be careful not to over-apply inorganic fertilizers. High concentrations of nutrients in the soil can harm a plant. Also, if not used by the plant right away, these inorganic nutrients tend to get washed out of the soil when the plant is watered so over-applying them can be wasteful. I find it best to use water soluble inorganic fertilizers in small amounts on a regular basis instead of a few 'big hits' over the course of the season. You can also purchase inorganic slow release fertilizers to add to container soils that will release nutrients into the soil over a longer period of time.

Organic fertilizers are derived from natural animal, plant and mineral sources. The nutrients in these sources are locked into organic compounds and they must be freed by microorganisms before the nutrients will be available for your plants to use. Organic fertilizers contain a wide array of macro and micronutrients. The concentration of nutrients in organic fertilizers is quite a bit lower than in inorganic fertilizers and the concentrations can vary greatly between batches of fertilizer. Many commercially available organic fertilizers are blends of several other organic fertilizers, mixed together to create a balanced fertilizer product.

Fertilizers on the Balcony

I mix a good amount of compost into my potting soil at the start of each season to provide my plants with a good mix of macro and micronutrients. However I've found that adding too much compost to a potting soil makes it overly dense. I would guess that I never add more than 30% new

Organic Fertilizer	Description	Provides
Blood Meal	Water soluble slaughterhouse by-product.	Nitrogen
Bone Meal	Ground up bones	Phosphorous, calcium
Crab Meal	Ground up crab shells	Nitrogen, phosphorus, calcium
Compost	Decomposed organic matter	Various nutrients and microorganisms
Cottonseed Meal	Cotton industry by-product	Nitrogen
Feather Meal	Chicken processing by-product	Nitrogen
Fish Emulsion	Fish processing by-product in liquid form	Primarily Nitrogen but also other nutrients
Fish Meal	Dried, pressed and ground fish	Primarily Nitrogen but also other nutrients. More potent than fish emulsions
Greensand	Marine sediment	Potassium
Guano	Seabird and Bat droppings	Nitrogen and phosphorous
Kelp or Seaweed Meal	Collected from the ocean. Available in dry and liquid concentrate forms	Potassium, Nitrogen and various micronutrients
Shrimp Meal	Ground up dried shrimp shells	Nitrogen, phosphorus, calcium
Worm Castings	Worm droppings	Various nutrients and microorganisms

Various organic fertilizers and what they provide

compost to my potting soil. And much of that tends to contain a fair amount of peat and humus to begin with. To provide my plants with even more nutrients I add a general purpose dry granulated organic fertilizer. I like to mix a good amount of this into each container. I've also used other organic supplements such as fish emulsions, kelp extracts and seabird droppings, to give the plants an extra boost. Because these fertilizers are organic, the nutrients are not immediately available and will be released into the soil as the fertilizer breaks down over a long period of time: perhaps an entire season.

Plants can absorb small amounts of nutrients through their leaves and some gardeners like to spray their plants with a diluted fertilizer solution to provide them with more nutrients. This is known as foliar feeding and I've never done this myself. I'm not convinced the extra effort would provide me with noticeably better results. And I prefer to keep the leaves of my plants dry to prevent mildew.

I have used synthetic fertilizers in the past: the kind you mix into the water once a week. They certainly give good results and for the quantities I require I find it to be much cheaper than buying compost and other organic additives. But personally I've found there is something less satisfying about using the these inorganic fertilizers so I try to stay away from them. I have found I can achieve fairly decent results without them.

If you are just getting into container gardening and not sure what fertilizer to use, stick with a general-purpose well-balanced fertilizer for all of your containers. Something with somewhat equal amounts of the primary macronutrients is fine. And use the product as recommended on the package. After you become more comfortable with the other aspects of container gardening you can start experimenting with different fertilizers to discover what works best for you and your garden.

Nitrogen For Free

Legumes such as peas and beans are able to pull nitrogen out of the atmosphere. These plants are known as nitrogen fixers and this means that the roots of these plants have the ability to extract nitrogen from the atmosphere and store it in a form that is available for the plant to use when needed. For this reason there is a common belief that growing legumes is good for your soil. But consider this:

- There needs to be an abundance of a bacteria known as rhizobia present in the soil for this process to take place. No rhizobia, no nitrogen. I would not assume this to be present in your container soil unless you put it there (which you can).

- The nitrogen is fixed to the roots of the plant and legumes consume large amounts of nitrogen. Although some of that nitrogen might leach out into the soil, most of it is going to be used by the plant.

- To return nitrogen to the soil, let the plant die so the roots can start to break down and release unused nitrogen. Pulling the plants at the end of the season will take whatever unused nitrogen is left with them.

If you want to make the best use of the nitrogen your bean and pea plants are storing, at the end of the season cut the plants down and leave the roots in the soil over the winter. Or, if you have access to one, put the entire plant, roots and all, into a composter.

Compost

Compost is decomposing organic matter that is rich in nutrients. Bacteria, fungi and other microorganisms feed on decomposing matter, releasing nutrients and eventually converting the material into humus. It is the best thing you can add to your potting soil. When you put compost in your soil, the compost continues to break down and release nutrients. This process of decomposition can take anywhere from a couple of months to years to complete. You can easily set up your own system for creating compost or purchase it from a number of sources.

Where to get it

Making compost isn't difficult but making enough of it requires lots of space and effort. The alternative for those of us with space constraints or without time and patience, is to buy it. If you are lucky you might be able to find someone offering high-quality kitchen compost for sale or trade. If not, shop around and you will likely find big bags of stuff labeled "compost" at your local garden center.

The quality of compost available at garden centers is touch and go. Always start by reading the label. The stuff I find is typically only 1/3 compost. The other parts are peat and humus. Not a terrible mix really. Some materials used in commercially available compost include municipal waste (grass clippings and leaves), mushroom growing materials (straw), shrimp shells and seaweed. Each has its merits and the best compost is derived from multiple sources.

Stay away from bags of compost that are heavy with moisture. Some garden centers will store pallets of bagged compost outside exposed to the rain. True to its nature, the contents of these bags will suck up that moisture like a sponge and being stored in a plastic bag with little drainage, it will hold on to that moisture. All that excess water suffocates the organic life that lives in the compost, diminishing one of the key benefits of using compost in the first place. To make matters worse, being stored outside also means the bags get baked in the sun and that's not good either.

Municipal compost is another source to consider. In my city it is available for free in the spring. Check with your municipality to see if it is available and when. But be sure to find out where it came from before loading up the trunk of your car with it. These programs typically produce a low quality compost that may not be suitable for growing vegetables.

Overly moist compost from a bag will squish in your hand like muck.

Composted animal manures are very rich in nutrients. They come form animals like chickens, sheep, cows and horses. Mixing composted animal waste into my containers doesn't appeal to me. Apart from pelletized chicken manure and seabird guano, I've mostly avoided composted manures. If you do want to purchase manures, make sure they are sufficiently aged and ready for garden use. Otherwise you risk contaminating your harvest with deadly pathogens like E-coli and salmonella

If you have a small space and decide to make your own compost you will likely not generate enough for your gardening needs and you will need to purchase more to make up the difference. But even producing a small amount of your own compost can be rewarding. In a small space it is possible to compost small amounts in batches. In the fall I sometimes let my plants die and dry out and then I strip them and dump the bits into a 5 gallon bucket with some kitchen scraps. I let it all break down through the fall and winter and into the spring. It doesn't produce much compost but it doesn't take that much effort either and in this case it certainly doesn't take up much space.

Composting on the Balcony

To set up your own composter you don't need much more than a 5 gallon plastic bucket with some holes drilled in the bottom for drainage and a cover with some holes for ventilation. If you have a tight-fitting lid you can mix your compost by tilting the bucket and rolling it around. Otherwise you'll need a small rake or pitchfork to routinely mix it all up. Be sure to put something under the bucket to catch run-off. I just place mine on top of a container of potting soil I'm not using.

There are two ways to fill such a composter. You can fill the entire bucket in one batch and let it rot or you can continuously add to the bucket and when it gets full, stop adding and start turning. This way you start off with a continuous composter but turn it into a batch composter when it reaches capacity. To fill the composter all at once you need to have all materials on hand when you start so you might have to stockpile some things for a while before you can get started. But with such a small composter that shouldn't be a problem.

Materials used for composting fall into one of two categories: green and brown. Green materials are high in nitrogen and brown materials are high in carbon. Some green materials include kitchen waste, grass clippings, coffee grounds and plant cuttings. Dried leaves, paper, cardboard, straw and sawdust are examples of brown materials. Don't bother with plant stems or branches. They take too long to break down. Keep meats and animal waste out of the mix.

There is an ideal mixture of green and brown materials that will provide the best temperature and moisture for your composter. The ideal ratio is 30 parts carbon to 1 part nitrogen. But for small-scale composting on the balcony I wouldn't worry too much about hitting the ratio exactly. As a general rule, equal weights of brown and green will get you pretty close to a 30:1 ratio. And in my case that means dried leaves and kitchen scraps.

Start with a layer of brown material and then add all your greens and cover with the rest of the brown. The more broken up the material is, the faster it will decompose. Anytime you add new green material to the composter, cover it with a layer of brown. You should add a bit of water to the batch to get things started but not too much. You need to keep the contents damp but not soaking wet. If you keep it covered you should not need to add more water again for a while. A moisture imbalance means conditions for microorganism growth will be impeded. Too much moisture leads to too little oxygen. On the other hand too much oxygen leads to less heat and the process of decomposition will take longer.

It is important to keep mixing the contents every few days to aerate the batch. As the materials break down they give off heat but nothing significant in a batch this size. It will not be enough to sterilize the batch and certainly not enough to keep the batch from freezing solid through a cold winter. If it all freezes in the winter, don't worry about it. It will thaw in the spring and continue to break down for you then.

When you remove the lid you should instantly notice a decaying aroma but it shouldn't be offensive. Sometimes when mixing the bucket you may disturb a clump of matter at the bottom that missed getting mixed previously and this will smell nasty at first but within a day of being mixed, the bad smells will dissipate.

When it is ready, the compost will be dark brown in colour with no remaining un-rotted bits and it will smell earthy; not at all like rotting garbage. It will take several months for the material in your batch composter to break down. The exact amount of time depends on what initially went into the composter and outside temperatures.

Vermicomposting

Worm composting or vermicomposting involves the use of worms to consume and break down organic matter. Their excrement, known as worm castings, contains nutrients that make it an excellent plant fertilizer. Worm castings also contain worm mucus that helps the castings retain moisture. When the mucus around these castings hardens it prevents them from quickly breaking down in your potting soil, making the castings act like a slow release fertilizer. All of these properties make worm castings an excellent soil amendment.

Setting Up a Worm Bin

A vermicomposter or worm bin is a great way to compost kitchen waste in a small space such as a balcony. It can produce usable compost in a very short amount of time. Worm bins do not typically smell bad and require little maintenance. With a bit of planning you can even maintain them indoors if you have the space.

You can purchase some really nice worm bins. Some have multiple levels to make harvesting castings a breeze. But you don't need anything fancy to get started. Vermicomposting can be carried out using a container as simple as a storage tote. The container you choose should have a snug fitting lid. Drill a number of small holes in the lid for ventilation. The worms can fit through fairly small openings but will likely only attempt to break out when motivated to do so. In the container, drill some holes in the sides for ventilation and a number of holes in the bottom for drainage. Use a large tray under the bin to catch run-off.

Red wigglers, ready for action

Now you need some worms. Red wigglers (*Eisenia fetida*) are the way to go. Unlike other earth worms, these will eat their food where they find it. They do not burrow very deep. Red wiggler worms can consume their weight in food every day (half bedding, half organic waste). All they need is a damp dark place to do it in. You may have to mail order them and they are sold by the pound. If you want to start small, that's perfectly fine. Over time, if conditions are right and food abundant, the colony will multiply.

You need to provide a bedding material for your worms and they will consume this as well as the food you provide. Use a high-carbon bedding material to offset the high-nitrogen content of the worm food. Some suitable bedding materials to use are: shredded newsprint (not glossy or coloured), cardboard, dry leaves, dry grass clippings, chopped hay or straw, saw dust and peat moss. Never use coloured or glossy paper for bedding. Newsprint inks can make a real mess when wet but the inks are soy-based and apparently non-toxic. If using peat moss, use it in moderation with other bedding materials as its lower pH will create an undesirable environment for the worms.

Start by filling your bin to 1/3 capacity with damp, wrung out bedding. The bedding should be damp but not soaking wet. Worms need to keep their skin moist to survive and suffocate in arid environments. However too much moisture is not good for the worms either. Fluff it up so there are no dense clumps in the bin.

When you turn your worms out into the bin, do so in a well-lit place and the worms will very quickly wiggle their way into the bedding to escape the light. Give them a day to adjust to their new home before feeding them for the first time. The worms are most content when temperatures are between 60 and 77°F (15 and 25°C). Keep the bin in a shady, well-ventilated place out of the sun to avoid overheating.

Worm Food

With everything set up and ready to go you can start adding food. As with composting, feed your worms a balanced diet of greens (food scraps) and browns (the bedding in the bin) to obtain the best mix of nutrients. Avoid overly-moist foods, such as melons. The added moisture can make the bedding in the bin too wet. The worms will appreciate a complex carbohydrate from time to time, such as a piece of stale bread.

You should also add some garden soil to the bin that the worms can use in their stomachs as grit. This needs to be real garden soil and not potting soil. The worms will consume this and it will help them digest their food.

Start by feeding the worms small amounts at first: no more than they can consume in a couple of days. Less and more often is always better than lots all at once. Chop their food into small pieces. The smaller the better. Pull back some of the bedding and add their food off to one side of the bin. Be sure to cover the food with bedding to prevent it from smelling bad as it decays and to discourage flies and insects from raiding the bin. You might have to add more bedding over time. I find a spray bottle helps to add moisture to the bedding if it starts to dry out.

Be careful not to over feed your worms. Too much food will just decay and generate heat which is not good for the worms. And all that extra food adds extra moisture to the bin also. If the worms are not happy with their environment they will try to find a way to leave it. Do not be too concerned about not feeding your worms enough. Remember that they also eat their bedding. They will not starve right away.

Over time, the worms will have converted a good amount of their bedding along with the organic matter you've provided into castings. When you can easily see the castings in the bedding it is time to consider harvesting them. Under typical conditions in a storage-tote sized bin it can take several months before you have a good amount of castings to harvest.

Harvesting Castings

Dump part or all of the contents of the bin into another bin or onto a drop sheet and start separating worms and uneaten bedding and food from the castings. Since the worms migrate to areas of the bin containing food, if you've alternated feedings from one side of the bin to the other you should be able to scoop out the contents of the inactive side of the bin without catching too many worms in the process. This smaller amount of material will be easier to sift through for wigglers and unprocessed material. Also watch for egg cases while harvesting. Don't toss these out. Egg cases are very small, about the size of an apple seed, and start out yellow in colour and turn brownish red before hatching.

Worm-tea is a nutrient rich liquid made by leaching nutrients out of worm casting. The run off you collect from the bottom of your worm bin IS NOT worm tea. This is simply a leachate released from the worm food as it decays and it should be discarded. It has virtually no nutrient value and under extreme cases can be toxic to your plants.

Winter Survivability

I live in a cooler climate and by late fall it starts to get frosty on my balcony. Red wiggler worms cannot survive freezing temperatures and a worm bin will not provide enough insulation or heat to keep the worms alive through the winter. Although you can keep a worm bin indoors and lots of people do, it can produce a certain noticeable aroma that you may not be comfortable with. And if you don't keep the food that goes into the bin properly covered it can smell like rotting garbage at times. I have absolutely no space in my home to maintain a worm bin and for that reason I have not been able to maintain a worm bin year round. But if I had access to a basement or heated garage, I would likely have a worm bin there now!

Getting Your Plants Started

In northern climates, to get the most out of the growing season some plants will need to be started indoors. Purchasing starter plants from a garden center or growing your own indoors from seed will give you a head start and extend your growing season by a few weeks. For people in areas with shorter growing seasons this is the only way to grow some vegetable crops to maturity.

Some plants are very difficult to grow from seed. Plants with very tiny seed can be difficult to plant and some seeds have strict germination requirements and never seem to get a proper start outdoors. On the other hand, some plants simply do not transplant well and the only way to grow these plants is to buy seeds and plant them directly into the container in which you plan to grow them to maturity.

Vegetables to Transplant

Broccoli	Eggplant	Pumpkins
Cauliflower	Melons	Squash
Cucumber	Peppers	Tomatoes

Vegetables to Direct Sow

Beans	Swiss Chard	Potatoes
Beets	Lettuce	Radish
Carrots	Peas	Spinach

Those listed above that are recommended for transplant can also be directly sown outdoors if your growing season is long enough.

The most important thing, whether you start from seedlings or seeds, is knowing when to start planting. The last frost date is a date in the spring after which the risk of frost has past. There is always a possibility for a late frost after this date but it's not typical. For fall crops you need to know your first frost date. This is the date for when you can expect the first frost in the region. The exact dates will vary from year to year and different sources will likely provide you with slightly different dates.

If you know your plant hardiness zone, you should be able to find rough estimates for those dates. For me, the last frost date I use is May 9 and the first frost date is October 6. When in doubt, ask someone at a nursery or garden center or consult the Internet.

Plant	Seed to Maturity (days)	Seed to Transplant (days)	Transplant to Maturity (days)	Plant out from last frost
Basil	80	40	40	+ 2 weeks
Bean - Bush	60	-	-	+ 2 weeks
Beans – Pole	60	-	-	+ 2 weeks
Beets	60	-	-	On last frost date
Broccoli	120-150	50	70-100	- 2 weeks
Cape Gooseberries	120-140	60	60-80	+ 2 weeks
Carrots	90	-	-	On last frost date
Cucumber	60-90	20	40-60	+ 4 weeks
Eggplant	120-150	60	60-90	+ 4 weeks
Kale	60	-	-	-2 weeks
Lettuce	60	20	40	- 2 weeks
Parsley	90	60	30	+ 2 weeks
Peas – Bush or Snap	60	-	-	- 2 weeks
Peppers	120-150	60	60-90	+ 4 weeks
Potatoes (Early)	90	-	-	- 2 weeks
Pumpkin	120-150	20	100-130	+ 4 weeks
Radish	30-60	-	-	- 2 weeks
Spinach	50	-	-	-2 weeks
Strawberries	80	30	50	On last frost date
Swiss Chard	60	-	-	- 2 weeks
Tomato - Indeterminate	120-150	60	60-90	+ 2 weeks
Watermelon	100-120	20	80-100	+ 4 weeks

Typical growing times for some common garden herbs and vegetables

Seed companies will usually provide a "days to maturity" count for their seed which is the number of days it will take under ideal conditions for the seed to grow into a plant that produces something that is ready to harvest. In some cases, the days to maturity count will refer to the time to reach maturity from transplanting. You will need to know these times as well as your frost dates to determine the best time to start your crops.

It is a good idea to record when you started every plant in each of your containers, tracking their growth and when they were ready for harvest. This can take a lot of the guess work out of planning your garden in the seasons to come.

Purchasing Seedlings

I'm always amazed at how strong and healthy the starter plants look at the garden centers in the spring. And why shouldn't they? They are grown under ideal conditions, ready to be sold and transplanted. It helps to shop around when looking for plants to start with but keep in mind that these plants are only offered for sale for a limited time. Selecting good candidates for your garden is mostly a matter of looking for strong healthy plants that are stocky, growing upright and without disease or pests.

Rarely have I bought starter plants from a garden center that were not root bound with a mass of roots circling around and around in their tiny plastic containers. When you plant these, you will have to gently free some of the roots so the plant doesn't remain root bound after being transplanted. A root bound plant will not be able to send new roots into the soil. If the roots are bound too tight, you'll actually have to rip some of this root mass away. This will shock the plant and it may take a while for it to recover after being transplanted..

Watch out for insects on your new plants, specifically aphids, spider mites and whiteflies. It only takes a few to start an invasion on your balcony. If you spot them after you've brought your plants home, inspect the plants carefully and deal with the problem immediately. I've made the mistake of purchasing plants that were so badly infested I would have been better off not buying them at all.

Young plants that are flowering or fruiting will not necessarily give you a head start. The flowers will likely drop off when the plant is transplanted. If the temperatures are still too cool outside, the flowers will not properly pollinate or set fruit. If this early flower or fruit does grow to maturity, it will likely be stunted. It will also inhibit the plant from growing bigger and producing a larger crop. It takes a lot of energy for a plant to set fruit and make seeds and in the early stages of life you want your plants to focus that energy on growing infrastructure instead: stems and leaves. Only after the plant has established itself should it be allowed to devote its resources to seed production. I usually pinch off these early flowers on baby pepper and tomato plants.

Early flowering and extreme root mass in seedlings from garden centers is a sign of over-stimulation (or just the right stimulation, depending on how you look at it). Nurseries devote lots of resources to growing seedlings. They provide them with ideal temperatures, light, moisture and lots of nutrients and growth stimulants to get the plants looking their best for the spring gardening rush. Healthy seedlings have a better chance at survival after transplanting which translates into a happy customer and a healthy cash flow for the nursery.

There are some plants that should be started from seed that you might still find for sale at garden centers as starter plants. Anything with a large tap root will not be happy with transplanting. A tap root is a single root that grows deep into the soil from which other secondary roots emanate. Some plants start out by growing tap roots but over time grow additional roots to form a fibrous or branched root system. Plants with a fibrous root system have an easier time recovering from and surviving a transplant. Carrots and other such root vegetables are examples of plants with tap roots.

Purchasing Seeds

The advantage of buying seeds over starter plants is that you have a much larger variety of plants to choose from. Most of the garden centers I visit don't sell much variety when it comes to seedlings; maybe three or four different tomato varieties for example. But I have a seemingly endless selection of seeds to choose from through online seed sellers.

Seed catalogs always seem to come in the mail during the depths of winter, long before you need to be planting seed. It's easy to be swayed by the glowing recommendations and colourful images of lush plants producing basket loads of perfectly shaped vegetables! Truth is, seed catalogs are marketing tools for the seed companies and the descriptions in those catalogs are written to sell you seed so try not to be swayed too much by the reviews and recommendations within the seed catalog pages.

Nearly all of the seeds I plant I purchase online. One company I used to buy from would sell seed packets with as few as 10 seeds in them. The per seed cost was obviously higher than buying in larger quantities but for me, 10 seeds of an heirloom tomato or pepper plant is enough for two seasons.

Seeds have a limited shelf life. Most will only be viable for 3 to 5 years. Even in their first year, germination rates can be as low as 80%. Store your seeds in a cool dry place. Most packets will be stamped with a "sow by" date or a packaging date. As the seeds age, fewer and fewer will germinate. If you're uncertain whether or not your seeds will germinate, dampen some paper towel and fold it a few times around a dozen seeds. Place this in a sealed container such as a jar or sealable plastic bag and place it in a dark, warm place. Check on the seeds every now and then to see if any have germinated and compare the time to germinate with the time given on the seed packet.

Heirlooms versus Hybrids

Heirloom varieties of plants are those that have not been altered by hybridization. They grow from seed as they would have since way back when. Heirloom varieties are propagated through open pollination (natural means) and to remain pure the seeds must come from plants that have been pollinated with pollen from the same plant variety.

Cross-pollination is the process of pollinating flower with the pollen of a flower from another variety of the same plant. The resulting seed will result in a new hybrid plant. Plants are bred this way to form new varieties of plants with traits that make them more desirable such as resistance to disease, tolerance to different climate conditions, or perhaps fruit of a particular colour. I sometimes grow hybrids but whenever I can I grow heirloom varieties, preferably from organically produced seed from small local producers.

Genetically modified (GM) plant varieties are grown from seed that has been genetically modified to be superior in some way. This involves the introduction of foreign genes into the seeds. For example, splicing genes from a deep sea fish into the genes of a tomato might create a tomato plant resistant to cold climates. Genetically modified corn and canola are big GM crops. The companies that produce these seeds retain patent rights to the new seed and therefore anyone growing their seeds who does not have the right to do so (through purchase of the seed from licensed sources) can be prosecuted. This is very different from heirloom seed which is considered "public domain" and free for everyone to use and propagate. I have yet to come across garden vegetable seeds that are genetically modified but I won't be too surprised if they show up in seed catalogs someday soon.

Starting with Seeds Indoors

I've been starting plants from seed in my kitchen window for as long as I've been gardening on my balcony. All you need is some good sunlight and a bit of air circulation. Avoid an overly hot window sill and shield the containers to prevent the soil in them from being cooked into a brick by the sun. I occasionally use fluorescent growlights for supplemental lighting.

Find Suitable Containers

There are an infinite number of containers out there that you can recycle for seed-starting purposes. Just be sure to punch a few holes in the bottom of them for drainage. You can also reuse what your starter plants from the garden center came in last season. I never seem to have enough of those around when I need them. More recently I've been using special reusable seed starting trays.

Collection of recycled containers to be used for seed starting

There are advantages to using pots made from bio-degradable materials such as peat, coir, paper, compressed soil and manures. When the seedling is large enough, you can pot the whole thing, container and all, directly into the soil. This is particularly useful for starting plants that don't like to be transplanted because you won't have to disturb the plant's roots.

Roots tend to grow through the walls of these bio-degradable containers and when the root tips are exposed to the dry air they dry out and stop growing, forcing the plant to create more roots in the container. This is known as air pruning and it is a technique used to create transplants with denser and healthier root systems. Plants started in plastic containers and left there too long will have a tendency to create long roots that spiral around inside the container.

I've used peat based starter containers in the past and if kept wet enough, roots certainly will grow right through the wall of the container. Mold usually forms on the walls of these containers as they are always damp but it has never caused me any trouble. I find that the pots don't break down quickly after transplanting and I get the feeling that in some cases, they actually prevent the plant from quickly sending new roots into the new container. I usually rip the bottom and sides off the these pots to free the roots before transplanting which kind of defeats the purpose of using in the first place.

root bound   air pruned roots

Some plants will need to be transplanted to a larger starter container after they have outgrown their initial starter container. Tomatoes are good examples of plants that benefit from being potted up before being transplanted outside. Tomato seeds can be started in seed trays and once they grow to the point where their roots fill the cells in the tray, transplant each of them into their own small container where they will have space to grow a little more while they wait to be moved into their permanent home.

Choose a Suitable Soil for Seed Starting

To grow your own starter plants you should start with a sterile potting soil or one that is specifically marketed as being ideal for seed starting. They tend to be a little finer and don't contain the same amount of fertilizers and nutrients. They are little more than a growing media in which the seeds can safely sprout and they contain very little to nourish the plant beyond a few weeks of growth.

For seed-starting, I always use a new bag of potting soil. Go through what ever potting soil you plan to use for seed starting and remove any sticks, rocks or hard clumps. Potting soils need to be damp before use but not soaking wet. A good bag of fresh potting soil will usually be pre-moistened.

Planting Your Seeds

Fill the containers to within 1/2 inch from the top. Watering newly planted seeds can wash the seed further into the soil so I like to water the soil in the container before I plant the seeds. This also helps to settle the potting soil into the container.

Place 1,2 or 3 seeds on the soil surface. For larger seeds you should make a small depressions in the soil with something like a pencil, and put a seed in each hole. Stick to the recommended planting depth printed on the seed packet. Some seeds prefer to germinate on the soil surface in the presence of light. Cover the seeds lightly with more soil or vermiculite if you have it available and lightly mist or water this newly added soil.

Make sure everything is labeled properly. I once had four varieties of pepper started and didn't label them. When they came up, they all looked the same and I very quickly forgot which one was which.

Water

When watering newly seeded containers, be careful not to water them so much that the seeds are washed into the soil and displaced. And resist the urge to over-water or your seeds and seedlings will rot. Your watering goal is to prevent the seed or seedling from drying out, not to keep them constantly soaking wet. Seeds that haven't sprouted do not need constant watering.

A capillary mat is a useful tool for assisting with watering seedlings. One end of the mat is placed in a tub of water and slowly it will wick up the water, making the entire mat wet. The seedling containers placed on the mat should have large holes in them so the potting soil in them is always in contact with the mat. As long as the mat remains moist, the potting soil in the containers will wick up the moisture and also remain moist and the seedlings will have a continuous but moderate source of moisture. There are seed starting trays available which incorporate a built-in water reservoir and capillary mat for watering.

Warmth

Different seeds have different temperature requirements for germination. For most, room temperature will be good enough although providing a little extra heat will really give some seedlings a boost, particularly heat-loving plants like tomatoes and peppers. You can purchase heating mats to place under your seedlings to boost the temperature a few degrees but I don't find it to be necessary for the number of plants I usually grow. Some seeds prefer cooler temperatures but again, I just stick with room temperature and everything works out fine.

Light

When growing on a window sill with nothing more than sunlight for a light source, plants will grow tall and skinny if left too long. They need to be under better lighting to grow properly. And if your windows are heavily tinted your only option for indoor growing will be artificial lighting. When I start plants indoors without supplemental lighting I tend to put them out a little earlier to get them under stronger sunlight sooner.

Of course, if you have a proper growlight and growing station, lighting will not be a problem. You can also provide supplemental lighting using florescent strip lights. Standard cool white fluorescent bulbs will work but growlight bulbs provide an even better light source for growing plants. The seedlings must be a few inches below the light for best results. High output T5 fluorescent bulbs can provide quite a bit more light in less space than the old T12 or T8 bulbs. Especially when used in a fixture that has a reflector. I have also seen compact fluorescent growlight bulbs what will fit in a standard light socket. Prop up each individual or group of seedlings with something to get them close to the light. I find the seedling grow a little stronger and less spindly when provided with the extra lighting.

Most seeds germinate in the dark so don't bother putting them out in the sun before the sprouts have poked out above the soil surface. Have an idea of how long it should take your seeds to come up so you can start again if they don't germinate. In a window sill, with the sunlight streaming through the window, the soil in the little containers will dry out quickly and you will have to provide them with some shade. Place a strip of cardboard or foil in front of the containers so the sunlight does not heat up the soil too quickly. You must not let the seedlings dry out.

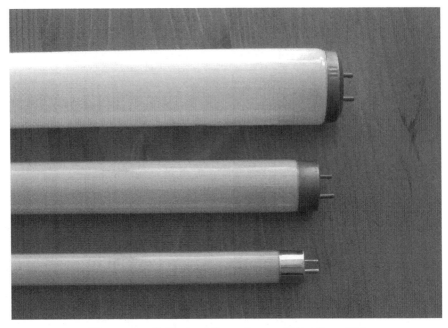

Fluorescent bulb sizes. From the top, T12, T8 and T5

Caring for New Seedlings

When the seeds start to sprout, if you've planted more than one seed in each container, pinch or cut off the weaker ones so you're left with just one seedling per pot. You can pull them out too but this can disturb the roots of the seedlings nearby that you want to keep. You should also provide some gentle air circulation around your seedlings. This will help prevent mold from forming on the damp soil surface and it will provide a bit of physical stimulation for the new plants, encouraging stockier growth. I like to pass my hand back and forth through the new plants whenever I pass by them to give them a bit of a workout to help strengthen their stems.

The first pair of leaves your seedlings put out are called cotyledons (or seed leaves). Seeds contain everything they need (except water) to sprout and get their starter leaves growing. The next set of leaves will look more like the leaves the plant normally grows and these are the first true leaves. After this stage you will need to apply a mild fertilizer otherwise the plants will grow weak and may drop leaves. If you notice the leaves turning a different shade of green then your new plants are in need of some nutrients. Water them using a diluted mix of water soluble fertilizer and do not over fertilize as this can cause more damage. When your seedlings reach the right size it will be time to transplant them into their permanent home.

Typically you can do this after they form their third or fourth true leaf although you may need to wait longer for the weather outside to cooperate.

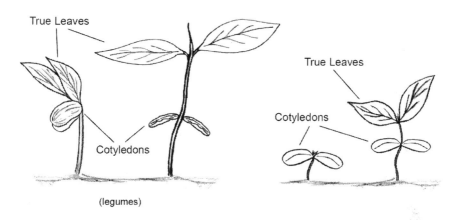

(legumes)

Transplanting your Seedlings

Before transplanting, seedlings should be "hardened off". They have been growing in a sheltered environment and to survive living outside they must get used to it first. Start by putting the seedlings outside for a couple of hours a day under partial shade and gradually increase their exposure to the outside world until they can tolerate a night on their own. Also cut back on their water to help toughen them up. The more time you can provide for this, the better. A week or two is ideal. My plants are living on the balcony 24 hours a day by the time I'm ready to transplant them.

The best time to transplant is in the morning when it is still relatively cool outside. When removing seedlings from their pots, I find that if the soil is too dry it will crumble away from the roots when the seedling is freed and if it is too wet it will slip away from the roots also. If the seedling is root bound, with the roots so thick that they form a mass that circles the inside of their container, gently loosen the roots before planting. You may have to cut some of this root mass away first. If its roots are bound too tight when transplanted, the plant will not be able to send out new roots and the plant will not grow properly.

Prepare your container and dig out soil from the spot you want to plant the seedling so that the root ball of the seedling will sit in the container at about the same level as it did in its starter pot. It doesn't have to be exact but some plants, like lettuce, will not tolerate being buried past their crown.

Fill in the gaps around the root ball, gently pack the soil and give it a good drink of water. After being transplanted it will take the plant a little while to re-establish a growing root system. Until then it will not be able to draw in a large amount of water from the potting soil. Protect newly transplanted seedlings from overheating by keeping them out of direct sunlight and strong winds for a while until they re-establish themselves.

Direct Seeding

Direct seeding, which is planting seeds outside into their permanent growing containers, is fairly straight forward. I find it helps if the potting soil in the container is thoroughly moist before I start seeding. Just put an indentation in the soil where you want to plant the seed, drop it in and cover it. Be careful not to plant the seeds too deep as they will take longer to sprout or worse, not sprout at all. Always consult the seed packet for depth and spacing requirements.

Water newly planted seeds gently. I find a spray bottle works great for the first little while until the seedlings break through the soil surface. But there is no need to constantly water them either. In fact, a thoroughly soaked seed will have all the moisture it needs to start germination. Initially, you should only be watering newly planted seeds to keep the soil from drying out.

If you plan to plant several plants in a single container, arrange them in a grid pattern and maintain equal distance from all neighbours. This will make good use of your space. For plants that need to grow up a trellis or fence, plant them in a row. If you are concerned about germination rates you can always seed two or more seeds at each location.

Germination temperatures quoted on seed packets refer to soil temperature, not the air temperature. Seeds planted when the temperatures are cool and the potting soil too moist will rot and fail to germinate. In the spring, the soil in earth based gardens will remain cold and damp for some time as it is still warming up after being frozen all winter. But this is not the case with potting soil in a container on your balcony.

Because your containers are above ground, the temperature of your potting soil will pretty much be the same as the surrounding air temperature, especially near the soil surface where your seeds are planted. If you are concerned about soil temperatures, you can purchase a soil thermometer to insert into your potting soil to test the actual temperature. Your container soils will heat up much quicker when exposed to the suns rays which can be an advantage or disadvantage depending on what you are trying to grow. Fortunately you can always move the containers into some shade if the sun's rays start to overheat them. And if you have the space, when it gets too cold at night, you can always bring the containers indoors.

Tomato seedlings, started in the kitchen and spending the days outside to harden off before being transplanted

The crown of this celery seedling is the part of the plant just above the soil surface from which the stems emanate

Sunlight

To grow good vegetables you need a good amount of sunlight. If you have too much, you can always find a way to create shade but on a balcony more often the problem is not having enough. And it doesn't take much of a shadow to drastically reduce the amount of sunlight your plants receive.

To maximize the amount of sunlight plants on your balcony receive you may have to arrange them in ways that make your balcony less accessible. The best place for sunlight will be at the edge of the balcony. If you have a solid railing or half wall at the outer edge, you will need to get your plants up higher to "see" the sun, or set them back a bit further from the edge.

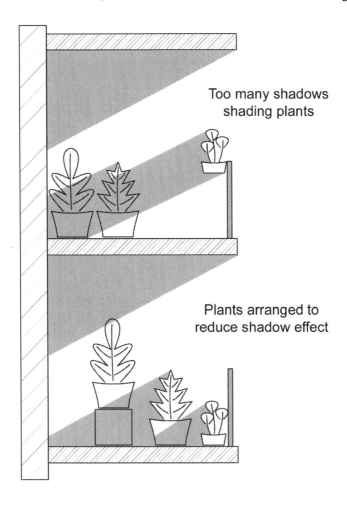

Too many shadows
shading plants

Plants arranged to
reduce shadow effect

If you are growing plants of equal height, it will help if the row of plants further back on the balcony are elevated so they are not living in the shadow of their neighbours in the front row. One nice thing about a balcony with an overhang is that it is shielded from rain and snow. So tables and shelves used to hold plants will not weather as quickly and should last longer.

With larger vining plants such as cucumbers and melons, a trellis is the best way to grow them. It keeps the vines off the balcony floor and up into the sunlight. The wider and taller the trellis is, the more the plant can spread out and space its leaves to collect the maximum amount of light. There are several dwarf or bush cucumber and tomato plants available that are said to be great for small spaces. But on a balcony like mine with a solid half wall around it, these bush varieties do not get enough light unless I prop them up a few feet. That's why I prefer the much larger vining varieties of tomato, cucumber and bean. I can train them to grow up a pole or trellis, 6 or 7 feet tall, where they can easily reach above my half wall and spread out to catch some sun.

Gardening in this manner is known as vertical gardening. It keeps plants from being stepped on and puts them up higher so you are not always bending over to inspect them or work with them. It also frees up your floor space.

Leave room for your plants to spread out and make the most of the available light. Plants placed too close to one another will receive less light and will not be able to grow out to catch the sunlight. Overcrowding also cuts down on air flow and circulation and in damp conditions this promotes the spread of mold and mildew. It is better to have fewer plants that can all receive the maximum amount of sunlight.

I've found that root crops and other low-lying plants grow best under overhead light so I like to place them where they can catch the sun as it passes over the balcony overhang. You can buy containers that hang on railings and I've seen brackets that can be purchased for hanging containers from the tops of railings also. I have a container with legs that reaches the height of my half wall and in this I sometimes grow root vegetables or other plants that I feel deserve better sunlight exposure.

Leafy plants and some herbs can manage alright in partial shade. In fact some burn easily in the hot afternoon sun and therefore do better with a little less sunlight. Parsley and chard are two that I've had no problems growing in partial shade conditions. Some plants that enjoy sunlight but not the heat, like lettuce and peas, can be started early in the year under direct sunlight and moved to partial shade once the plants mature. Plants that prefer cooler temperatures should be placed so that their containers are shielded from direct sun to prevent overheating. But heat-loving plants may benefit from having their containers gently warmed by the suns rays. Just keep an eye on them and don't let those containers dry out.

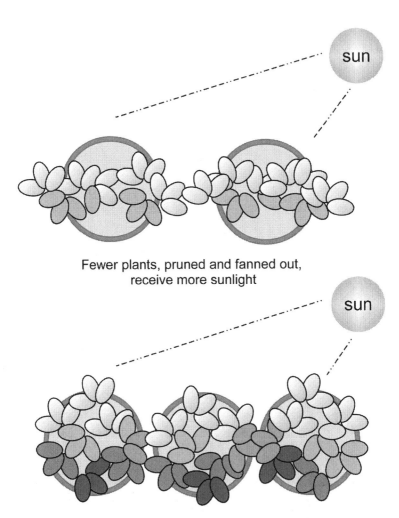

Fewer plants, pruned and fanned out,
receive more sunlight

More plants, crowded and unkept,
receive less sunlight

Providing Support

To keep everything growing upwards a little assistance is required. Anything that grows like a vine: indeterminate tomatoes, pole beans, melons, cucumbers, and peas, will all grow better on your balcony if you give them something to climb on. It keeps their fruit off the balcony floor and gets their leave up into the sunlight. Even compact busy plants will benefit from some added support on windy days.

I like using bamboo poles to support my container plants and over the years I've accumulated a nice bundle of them. You can create a simple temporary trellis with three upright poles stuck into a container of potting soil. Weave at least two horizontal poles between the uprights in such a way that they will stay in place on their own and you'll have a simple trellis. Bamboo is great for this thanks to its strength and flexibility. The poles can all be lashed together with cord, string, twine, garbage bag ties... whatever, to keep them from slipping out of place although they should be able to stay up on their own. Plastic cable ties also do a great job of keeping it all held together.

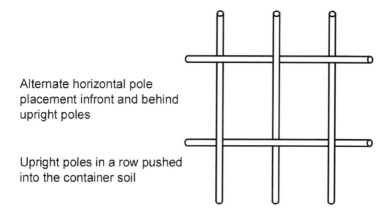

Alternate horizontal pole placement infront and behind upright poles

Upright poles in a row pushed into the container soil

I use bamboo in this manner to hold tall tomato plants. A stake cannot be driven deep enough into a container of potting soil to provide stable support. A large container-bound plant that starts swaying on a windy day can easily be toppled over. So in addition to a central pole, on each side of the container I add additional upright poles that I secure to the edge of the container and then I weave a couple of horizontal poles between the three upright poles. It's similar to a trellis but instead of using it for a vine to crawl and twist around I use it to provide something I can secure the tomato branches onto.

If you use plastic or wood containers and your support poles are next to the edge of the container, a pair of holes can be drilled through the container on either side of the pole so it can be secured to the container using a cable tie, cord or wire. This will prevent the pole from moving back and forth too much in the potting soil on windy days.

Some plants will not need anything other than a stick in the ground to lean on but others will need a little more help. And they will need to be secured to their support structure. You can tie plant stems up with just about anything, just be sure not to tie them too tight or you might damage and choke the plant. I recently started using strips of old rags to tie up my plants. They do not cut into the plants when you tighten them and best of all, they're free.

Sometimes you need to use something a little more substantial than a few poles stuck in the potting soil. You can purchase wood and metal trellises from garden centers but a good wind can easily blow such structures over. They must be anchored to something and drilling holes into your balcony or the surrounding walls may not be an option. I overcame this problem once by constructing a simple platform to sit a large container on and I used the platform as a base for a basic trellis

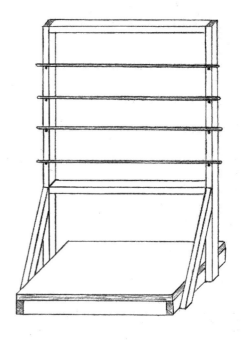

The whole thing was constructed from 1x2" furring strips and a 1/4 sheet of plywood and I probably could have done without the plywood. On the upright frame I used wood screwed to create mounting posts onto which I hung bamboo poles every 6 or 8 inches and I secured them with plastic cable ties. And I did it this way simply because these were the materials I had readily available. I'm sure there are an infinite number of ways to build such a system and all would be equally suitable. The important thing is that the trellis be anchored securely to the platform. With the entire structure held in place by the weight of the container, it's not going anywhere.

A strip of cloth used to tie a tomato to its support pole

You can use cable ties to secure poles to the sides of containers

A basic trellis attached to a platform held down by the weight of a container.

Water

Vegetables are thirsty plants. During summer's peak, each of my large self-watering containers will suck down a couple of gallons of water per day. These containers are usually potted with a pair of large tomato plants, a pumpkin or a watermelon: plants with lots of leaf surface. Where does all of that water go?

How Plants Use Water

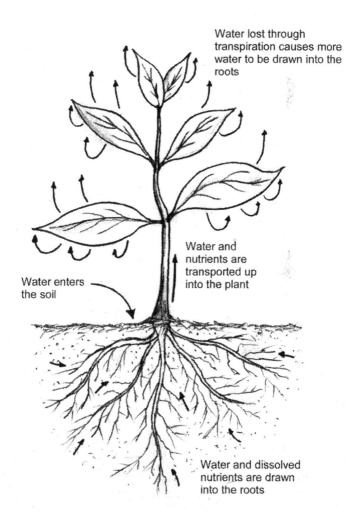

Water lost through transpiration causes more water to be drawn into the roots

Water and nutrients are transported up into the plant

Water enters the soil

Water and dissolved nutrients are drawn into the roots

Even on a warm sunny day, the leaves of a plant will feel somewhat cool to the touch. That's because water carried to the surface of the leaves will evaporate and this has a cooling effect. As moisture evaporates from the leaf surfaces (primarily the underside of the leaves), the plant begins a cycle that causes more water to be pulled up from the roots to replace the water that is evaporating. The flow of water into the roots, up the stems and off the leaves also transports nutrient from the soil up into the plant. This process is known as transpiration and it is what keeps the plant alive and growing.

Vegetable plants transpire profusely. Some of the water they drink is used to build plant material and is stored within the plant's cells. But over 90% of the water drawn in by a plant is lost to transpiration. The actual amount of water depends on the plant and its size, as well as air temperature and humidity. Hot, dry and windy conditions will result in a much higher rate of transpiration.

Watering Your Plants

Keeping container-bound vegetable plants properly watered can be a bit of a challenge. In the ground, plants send roots deep and wide to collect as much moisture as the can. Moisture deep in the ground beneath these plants does not readily evaporate. In a container, roots are limited to how far they can go to reach water. And the smaller volume of soil in a container means there is much less moisture available. Most vegetable plants thrive with a continuous supply of moisture during most of their life cycle. Yet typical container plants watered by hand receive a day's worth of water in a matter of minutes. Over the course of the day this water gets used up by the plant, evaporates off the soil surface or drains out the bottom of the container. So for part of the day, the plant is over-watered and for the rest of the day, the plant is dry and its roots vulnerable. It's a cycle you need to avoid when growing vegetables.

If your balcony is covered by an overhang your containers will not catch enough rain to keep your plants watered. So naturally, you'll be watering by hand. I have a large plastic watering can I use to water my plants that I fill in the kitchen sink and carry out to the balcony. During the summer I might have to do this 5, 6 or 7 times a day to get everything watered.

When I'm filling self-watering containers I use the watering can without a spray head attached. But for watering the soil surface of a container it is a good idea to have one. Too much water flow will compact the potting soil and disperse it at the surface, exposing plant roots.

I water my plants in the morning but on particularly hot days I sometimes need to add a bit more water to some containers again in the late afternoon. Common wisdom is to always water your plants in the morning. Temperatures in the morning are somewhat cooler and the sun is not at its peak so water will not evaporate away from the soil surface as quickly in the morning. This ensures your plants get a better chance at a good drink. But you can prevent some of this evaporation by covering the soil surface with a plastic mulch. And you can also shade your containers from the sun to keep them from over-heating.

It's easy to keep a self-watering container watered

Similarly, it is said that you should not water your plants in the evening or at night because water can remain on a plant's leaves. The cool darkness of the night provides an environment perfect for fungus and mildew development. However this is less of a problem in a balcony container garden where watering is not done with a hose or sprinkler. I try to avoid watering the leaves of my plants. Especially plants susceptible to mildew like cucumbers and melons.

Under-Watering

A plant wilting can be a sign that water transpiring from it is not being replaced fast enough. Plants wilt when too much water is drawn out of their cells. On hot days a bit of wilt is unavoidable but if you notice your plants wilting when the potting soil is still moist, the problem might not be with the amount of moisture in the soil but the ability of the plant to absorb it. The fine root hairs of a plant, the part of the root system that draws in moisture, die when they dry out which happens easily in containers exposed to lots of sunlight. This is particularly true if you use plastic containers as they provide no insulation against the heat of the sun. A plant with damaged roots will have a harder time getting the water it requires.

When plants do not receive the water they require they start preparing for seed production. The dry spell signals the end of the growing season and the plant rushes to fulfill its destiny and produce seed. In leafy plants this leaves us with a bitter tasting crop. Root vegetables get tough and woody when they don't receive enough moisture. However with fruiting plants you can use this to your advantage by backing off on watering when the plant has reached maturity to help coax it into fruiting. But letting a plant loaded with fruit dry out or wilt excessively will drastically reduce the flavor of the fruit on the plant and perhaps even ruin it.

Shallow Watering

When you water a traditional container, you add water to the soil surface. If you shallow water your plants by only soaking the top half or third of the soil in the container, your plant will suffer from a shallow root system. The roots will not grow deep enough to support the weight of the plant above the soil. They will not reach into the soil to make use of all available nutrients. And they will be more easily baked by the heat of the sun.

Shallow Roots

Deep Roots

The opposite of shallow watering is deep watering which is providing enough water to thoroughly soak the soil in the container. It is better to occasionally deep water your containers than it is to shallow water them often. Deep watering will create ideal root-growing conditions throughout the container soil, thereby promoting a larger and healthier root system. If you water the plant until water flows out the container drain holes, you know you've completely watered the container. Unfortunately, you also risk flushing nutrients out of the soil as well.

Over Watering

Even though they grow under the soil, the roots of a plant require oxygen. There is a balance that must be maintained between enough water and enough oxygen in the soil for plant survival. Over watering your plants will deprive their root systems of oxygen. Root tips grow into the tiny voids within the soil structure. These voids are normally filled with moist air and the roots need this to grow. When you water a container, the water should flow through the soil, filling the voids and eventually draining away, pulling air in behind it. But without proper drainage, excess water remains in the soil for too long and the root tips become oxygen-deprived and die. And just as with under watering, a plant with a damaged root system will have a harder time getting the moisture and nutrients it needs from the soil.

The solution is simply to provide more drainage holes and be mindful of how much water your plants are using. When it comes to water, more isn't always better.

A properly designed self-watering container doesn't require you to think too much about how much water to add or how often. For traditional containers, if you have a good number of drainage holes, knowing you've over-watered your plants will be obvious. It is also good practice to know how much your containers weigh when just watered. This way you can pick them up to get a feel for how much moisture is in the soil. The difference between a wet container and a completely dry one is quite significant.

When it is hot outside, resist the urge to over-water your plants. In the intense heat, plants will wilt and you may be tempted to water them thinking they have depleted their potting soil of all moisture and are in desperate need of more. But be mindful of how much moisture is already in the container soil before adding more. Adding more water to a container already full of moisture will not bring any relief to your plants and can do more harm than good.

Drip Irrigation

Drip or low-flow irrigation, also know as micro irrigation, is a watering system designed to provide just the right amount of water right to the plants. And it does so in a slow constant drip that provides the plant with a gentle but continuous supply of moisture. This helps avoid soil compaction and nutrient leaching. Once the system has been established, all you have to do is turn on the water supply for a set amount of time and let your irrigation system take care of watering your plants for you.

This dripper has a fixed flow rate of 1 gal/hr

On my balcony, like most high-rise balconies, I have no outdoor water faucet so most micro irrigation solutions will not work for me. However I have been able to set up a small irrigation system using a large bucket as a reservoir and use gravity to create a low-pressure flow of water. Obviously I have to fill this reservoir quite regularly. But the real problem is that most drip irrigation hardware such as drippers, sprinklers and timers require a minimum water pressure to operate and a little gravity-fed system will not provide the required pressure. The best way around this is to do away with using fancy irrigation hardware (which is expensive anyways) and just let gravity feed the water from the reservoir through flexible tubing right to the soil surface, without fancy drippers or sprinklers.

I once used a 5 gallon bucket to create my reservoir. At the bottom of the bucket I cut a hole and mounted a brass shutoff valve through the wall of the bucket with some rubber gaskets and plastic conduit locknuts. A hose adapter connected the valve to my 1/4 inch plastic waterline. My water supply line came from a drip irrigation kit. Flexible airline tubing like the kind used by aquarium hobbyists works great too but it kinks and pinches easily. Having a main valve to control the water flow helps but unless you are using drippers that regulate water flowing from them, you may find it necessary to restrict the flow on a plant by plant basis. Small plastic or brass airline valves, again, like those used by aquarium hobbyists, can be used to limit water flow. Or if you have the patience you can simply bend the waterline a little to pinch off the flow and use some tape to keep it pinched just right.

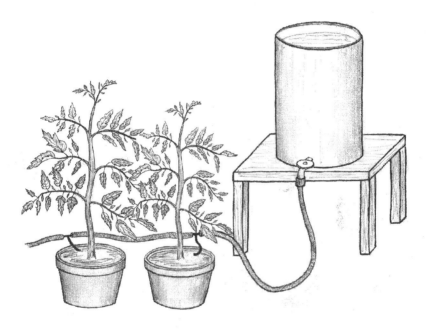

A little gravity- fed drip irrigation setup

If you don't want to spend the time sticking a value through a perfectly good bucket, water can also be siphoned out of the reservoir. Place one end of a water supply line into the reservoir well below the surface of the water and suck water out the other end of the line. As long as the exit end of the supply line is below the input end, water will continuously flow up over the edge of the bucket and through the waterline. The more water you have in the bucket, and the greater the difference in height between the output of the water line and input, the faster the water will flow. You can even block the output end completely and water will continue to flow again when you release it. Use multiple supply lines with one for each plant, instead of a single supply line with T's, to provide consistent flow to each plant.

There are some gravity fed drip irrigation kits and devices available that can make life easier. Some are nothing more than water bladders that can be hung above a plant with water traveling from the bladder through flexible tubing to the soil surface. Low-tech solutions like this are great for single plants that don't have large water demands. There are more expensive products that make use of battery-powered timers and electro-mechanical values that you can program to provide water from a table-top reservoir. They are expensive but can save you considerable time and guess work.

I am not a big fan of drip irrigation on the balcony. Without being able to rely on fixed-flow rate drippers or sprinkler heads, too much time is spent playing around to get the flow rates right. The other problem I have with a system such as this is that it doesn't let me easily move containers around on the balcony. And relying on gravity to deliver the water means the containers must always be below the water supply. I can't place them up on a shelf or table.

However, I have used drip irrigation to keep my plants watered for short periods of time while I was away on vacation. One thing I must stress about using any automatic watering system is to make sure you test it thoroughly before going on vacation. Set it up well in advance of your planned vacation time and let it run for a while. Give yourself lots of time to tune the system so it delivers the correct amount of water in your absence.

Self-Watering Containers

Self-watering containers are the best way to grow most vegetables on your balcony. What these containers do is provide a water reservoir at the bottom of the container where water can be wicked up by the soil above to keep it moist. As the plant draws moisture into its roots, water leaves the potting soil and this causes more water to be drawn from the reservoir into the potting soil to replace it. The advantage to you is that your plants will always receive water when needed, 24 hours a day, instead of all at once from your watering can. Self-watering containers avoid soil compaction because they don't need to be watered from the top. And nutrients don't get washed out the bottom of the container.

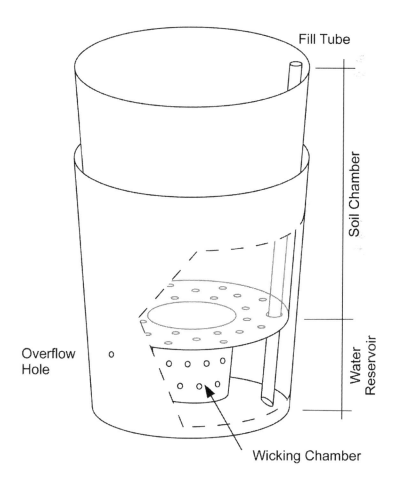

Anatomy of a simple do-it-yourself self-watering container

Not all plants appreciate self-watering containers. Many herbs prefer to be planted in containers that dry out from time to time. And just because it is a self-watering container does not mean you'll be spending less time watering it.

If you shop around you should be able to find suitable self-watering container systems for sale. But you don't need to be very handy to make your own. There are all sorts of plans on the Internet, even videos, with instructions for building one. At the very least you will need a pair of buckets, a plastic cup and something to cut holes through plastic.

Making A Simple Self-Watering Container

A very popular do-it-yourself self-watering container design uses a pair of 5 gallon buckets. Here's a list of everything you'll need:

- A pair of buckets

  Five gallon buckets, the kind used to hold everything from paint to pickles, work nicely. You can easily pick up a pair of clean 5 gallon buckets at any renovation or paint store. I also hear that large kitty litter pails work nicely too. The important thing is that they be stackable.

- Small plastic food container

  Large yogurt containers work for me. Anything about 4 or 5 inches in diameter and at least as deep.

- Electric drill with a 3/8 drill bit or something around that size

- Something to cut through plastic

  Jig saw, hack saw, hole saw... something to cut a larger hole in one of the buckets. You can also do this with the drill and a utility knife by drilling lots of holes close together in a circle and carefully using the utility knife to cut between the holes. Just be VERY careful with the utility knife – cutting a hole this way can be dangerous.

And optionally, to add a fill tube,

- A one or two inch diameter plastic tube or pipe at least as long as the bucket is tall

- Some cable ties, wire or cord.

You might need to get a bit creative with the instructions depending on the materials you have available but here is basically how you do it:

1. Select one of the buckets to be your inner bucket to hold potting soil and the other to be your outer bucket to hold water below the inner bucket.

2. On the bottom of the inner bucket, trace out and cut a hole big enough for the small food container to fit into. We'll call this container the wicking cup. If the wicking cup has a lip on it and you're good with a saw you might be able to cut the hole just right so the cup will rest in the hole perfectly without falling through the bucket. If not, that's ok. You can still make it work just fine.

   Note: It's always a good idea to wear safety glasses when working with power tools, even when cutting into something soft like plastic.

3. Cut several holes in the sides of the wicking cup so when it's filled with soil, water will freely flow in from the water reservoir and soak the soil in it.

The "wicking cup" is where the potting soil comes in contact with the water

4. Drill a bunch of small holes in the bottom of the inner bucket. Don't make the holes too big or all the soil will fall through but make sure there are lots of holes for good drainage. These holes will also help keep the roots at the bottom of the container aerated.

5. When you stack the inner bucket in the outer bucket it will probably sit too low to create a big enough water reservoir between the buckets. You can prop the inner bucket up with a couple more plastic food containers (like the ones you used for the wicking chamber) placed open end down in the bottom of the outer bucket. You should cut holes in them also so water can flow through them otherwise you'll be sacrificing some of your reservoir space. Alternatively you can drill pairs of holes around the outside of the buckets, above and below the rim of the outer bucket, and pass cable ties, cord or wire through the holes to fasten the two buckets together at the desired height.

Cable tie securing the inner bucket in position

6. Cut an overflow hole in the outer bucket at a point just below where the bottom of the inner bucket rests. If you don't plan to add a fill tube, make the hole is big enough to get the spout of your watering can through it. This is how you will fill your bucket.

And that's it – a basic self-watering container. Unless you've taken my cable tie approach to keep the inner bucket in place, wrap some packing or duct tape around the buckets at the rim of the outer bucket to keep them together. You might also need to wedge something between the two buckets, like a rag or wood shims, to keep the inner bucket centered.

If you want to make filling the water reservoir a bit easier you can add a fill tube. With this, you don't have to fill the container through the hole you cut through the outer bucket.

1. Cut the tube so it is long enough to sit well above the soil surface of the inner bucket and extend though the bottom of the inner bucket to rest on the bottom of the outer bucket.

2. Make a diagonal cut out of the end of the fill tube. This is the end to go through the bottom of the inner bucket. You do this so that when the tube is resting on the bottom of the bucket, water can freely flow out the bottom of the tube and into the reservoir.

3. Cut a hole in the bottom of the inner bucket near the outside edge for the fill tube to fit through.

4. Secure the fill tube to the inner bucket at its rim by drilling a pair of holes on either side of the fill tube. Pass a cable tie though the holes around the tube and fasten it. You could also use wire or string or whatever else you have handy.

A finished bucket with lots of drainage holes and a fill tube

Using the fill tube, you can add water more easily from the top of the container. And the original fill hole in the outer bucket can serve as an overflow, letting you know when you've added enough water and preventing you from flooding the container.

Another self-watering container constructed from a pair of storage totes

Using Your Self-watering Container

When you put potting soil in the bucket container, make sure the wicking cup at the bottom of the inner bucket is full of potting soil. If the gaps between the cup and the hole in the bottom of the inner bucket are too big you can stuff a rag into the gap to keep potting soil from slipping through. But don't be overly concerned if a bit of potting soil falls into your water reservoir. Now you can continue to fill the container with potting soil.

I've always used the same mix of potting soil in my self-watering containers that I use in my conventional containers. And I tend to fertilize them the same way also. I sometimes apply my fertilizer in a batch or band near the surface of the potting soil away from whatever I've planted in the container. And I then cover this fertilizer with an inch or two of potting soil. I use the same organic dry fertilizer I use with all my other containers. Nothing different.

Once you've planted something, give the container a good watering from the top first just as you would with a newly planted plant in a conventional container. Make sure the potting soil in the container is thoroughly moist and then fill the reservoir. To assist with moisture retention you can cover the top of the container with plastic because you no longer have to water the potting soil from the top of the container. If you still have the lid for the bucket you used to make your container you can cut holes in it for the fill tube and the plants and fit that over the container. I usually just wrap a garbage bag over the top of mine. Because your self-watering container waters your plants from the bottom up you will notice that the potting soil in the container remains loose and never compacts.

Keep an eye on the water level in the reservoir. You shouldn't need to add water to it for quite some time, until the plants in the container have expanded their roots and started using up the moisture in the potting soil. If the plants start to show signs of nutrient fatigue during the course of the season you can start topping up the reservoir with water mixed with liquid fertilizer. Use the same concentration you would add to your conventional container plants. There is also no reason why you can't add more dry fertilizer at the top of the container. I sometimes have to do this with my containers part way through the season.

A word of warning about keeping plastic containers in the sun: some plastics, particularly those not made to be kept outside, will break down when exposed to sunlight. It might take a while but eventually plastics kept outside for long periods of time will become brittle and will easily break. Certain plastic storage totes for example, will become weakened after a couple of years outside to the point where you can practically rip them apart with your bare hands.

Mulching Your Containers

To help conserve moisture in your containers, you can apply a mulch to the soil surface. The mulch slows the rate of moisture evaporation so you will not need to water your containers as frequently. Bio-degradable mulches can return some nutrients to the soil as they break down. You can use just about anything as a mulch: wood chips, straw, grass, newspaper, cardboard, pebbles... anything that doesn't compact and allows the soil to breathe. Avoid using materials that might leach something harmful into your potting soil.

Personally, I think mulching with wood chips and bark is a bad idea if you are growing vegetables in your containers. The mulch can easily get mixed up with the container soil and it takes a very long time to break down. And there is a belief that as the wood decomposes, nitrogen in you potting soil will be stolen and consumed by the bacteria breaking down the wood.

I sometimes use plastic to slow the rate of moisture evaporation from my containers. I use plastic garbage bags stretched over the tops of my containers with holes cut in the plastic for plants and watering. It's not pretty to look at but it works quite well and I don't need to worry about getting mulch mixed up with my potting soil. Covering your containers with plastic like this works best if you are using drip irrigation or a self-watering container; I find it is nearly impossible to get the container soil thoroughly moist when watering the container by hand through a hole in the plastic covering.

Plastic used to "mulch" a container

Maximizing The Harvest

There are several things you can do to increase the yield from your growing space. The plants you grow have one main desire in life and that is to reproduce. In some cases you will want to encourage this and in others, prevent it.

Some plants that we grow for their leaves will stop producing new leaves once they flower. Basil is a good example of this and I always pinch off the tops of my basil plants to discourage flowering. This also encourages branching and results in more leaf growth. In leafy green plants, changes in environmental conditions will cause them to bolt and start flowering. You can't do much about changes in temperature and sunlight, but you can keep these plants well-fed and watered to reduce stresses that simulate changing environmental conditions. This will help keep the plants from flowering prematurely.

For fruiting plants you will want to encourage and maximize flower production. Reducing the amount of water these plants receive at just the right time during the growing season will coax the plants into forming flowers and fruit to produce seed (see *Under-Watering* on page 57). You can provide these plants with fertilizers higher in phosphorous later in the season to encourages and support flower production. With plants you want to grow for their leaves, stick to a fertilizer that has less phosphorous to discourage flowering.

Optimizing Container Usage

To get the most out of your growing season, come up with a planting strategy that keeps all of your containers producing non-stop. Here are three things you can do to help maximize the use of your growing spaces.

- Inter-plant small, fast-growing crops with larger, slow-growing ones. Lettuce and radish plants grow fast and compact and they prefer cooler temperatures. You can seed a container with these smaller, faster growers along with larger slower-growing plants like tomatoes, knowing that the faster growing plants will be harvested long before they create problems for the larger slower-growing plants. Lots of leafy green plants like lettuce have shallow root systems and can be harvested on a cut-and-come-again basis so they never get too big. These are perfect to plant with larger deep rooted plants.

- Stagger your plantings. This is known as successive planting. If you were planting bush beans for example, instead of planting several containers all at the same time, start each container a week or two apart. Because bush beans tend to set a single crop all at once, by staggering the start of several plants you get a few smaller harvests spread out over time instead of one large harvest when all the plants mature at the same time.

- Reuse idle containers. Plants that finish early, like peas, will leave you with an idle container or perhaps part of a container. Fill the vacant space with something else. Perhaps use it to start some late season crops. Don't worry about nutrient depletion. Just add more fertilizer. Keep those containers producing.

When planting different plants in the same container, sometimes things don't turn out right and a plant you hoped would remain small ends up dwarfing and dominating its container mates. So experiment with spacing and timing to come up with a planting scheme that works for you. I've seen several recommended layouts and combinations for multi-crop containers that always look great when first planted. But in practice some of these recommended combo containers can be hard to keep under control.

Most things you grow will be happier in containers much larger than you can provide. For plants with deep growing roots like tomatoes, melons and squash, a deeper container will generally bring about greater yields. Smaller containers for large plants will mean more frequent watering and feeding. Your plants may not produce as much and will likely experience much more stress than those growing in an earth-based garden. But sometimes it makes more sense to sacrifice plant yield for balcony space. It's just not practical to maintain a container on your balcony with a 24 inch depth for the sole purpose of growing a tomato plant.

Companion Planting

Pairing up plants that nurture a symbiotic relationship with one another is known as companion planting. Small-scale organic gardeners like to practice companion planting almost religiously. Native Americans used to practice companion planting when growing their "three sisters": maize, squash and beans. They would plant several of each in large mounds. The maize in the center would provide support for the climbing beans and the large leaves of the squash would grow close to the ground, shading out the weeds and keeping the soil moist.

Plants that do not compete for growing space are good companions. A shallow-rooted plant will grow just fine when planted with a deep-rooting plant. Taller plants can be used as support for climbing plants, such as corn being used by pole beans and cucumbers. And ground cover crops are good for shading the soil to help prevent over heating and evaporation.

Grow plants together that do not compete for similar nutrients. Or grow plants that help improve the soil for their neighbours. Legumes that fix nitrogen from the atmosphere to their roots can help to bring some of this nitrogen to the soil for other plants. Some plants are thought to produce chemical compounds that negatively affect the growth of others nearby. Fennel is said to inhibit the growth of most vegetables planted near it. Some people believe that growing basil with tomatoes improves the taste of the tomatoes. Personally I think that's a bit of a stretch but tomatoes and basil certainly do taste good when eaten together, regardless of what they are grown next to!

Planting a crop that is used to deter pests from a more desirable crop is known as trap cropping. These trap crop plants trap the pests by attracting them and drawing them away from other vulnerable crops. Sometimes the plants just naturally act as a deterrent, such as onions that distract carrot fly. And some such as Marigolds or Nasturtium can be used to attract pests like aphids and keep them distracted.

A few flowers can go a long way to attracting beneficial insects to your balcony. Nasturtiums, which are also edible, are well respected as a companion plant for attracting predatory insects, as are dill and fennel. If you have free space or containers, consider planting a few marigolds, geraniums or nasturtiums. Even with help from these plants, you might still not attract enough beneficial insect visitors onto your balcony to make a difference, but at the very least the flowers will add some colour to your balcony.

Hand-Pollination

Most people with proper gardens don't have to worry about this much. But the semi-enclosed ecosystem you've created on your balcony is somewhat sterile when compared to gardens maintained at ground level and it is likely missing something crucial for the reproduction of many plant species: insects.

Some plants produce flowers that incorporate both male and female parts and are easily able to reproduce on their own. Tomatoes and peppers are two such plants. They produce what are known as perfect flowers and all they need to reproduce is a good shake from nothing more than a stiff breeze. But some plants such as melons, squash, cucumbers and pumpkins have separate male and female flowers and the pollen has to be transferred from the male flower to the female flower by a pollinator. In some cases the wind can accomplish this but most plant species rely on insects to help out with this task. When bees come around to collect nectar, flower pollen tends to stick to their bodies and is carried with them from flower to flower.

Chances are, you will not get very many bees on your balcony. Certainly not enough to guarantee that the half dozen female flowers your one watermelon or pumpkin plant produces will receive enough pollen to produce fruit. Instead of relying on insects, you should take matters into your own hands and pollinate the female flowers your self.

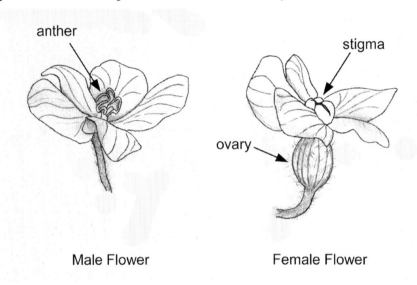

Male flowers have a stamen which consists of an anther connected to a filament that emanates from the base of the flower. Female flowers have a pistil which consists of an ovary at the base of the flower and extends along a tube like structure know as a style up to the stigma at the end of which is the receptor for pollen from the male anther. It is the ovary at the base of the female flower that will develop into whatever it is the plant is suppose to produce. And it is the anther on the end of the male stamen that carries the pollen needed by the ovary to turn it into a fruit.

Female flowers do not open for very long so it helps if you can identify them early and be prepared to service them as soon as they are ready. Over time you will get used to telling when a female flower is ready to open. Hand-pollination should be carried out in the morning when the female flowers are open and appear to be at their fullest. And with luck several male flowers will also be open and ready to do their part at the same time.

Transferring pollen from male to female flowers

Start by pulling an open MALE flower off the plant. Make sure you don't pull off a female by mistake! Don't bother with males that look like they are about to fall off or are not quite open yet. You need males with a generous coating of pollen. Pull the petals off the male flower to expose the anther which should be loaded with grains of pollen. With the male flower prepped, carefully wipe what you have left of it across the center of the female flower. Spread the pollen all over and around the stigma. Take your time and do a thorough job and do your best not to damage the female flower. If the pollen is not distributed evenly the fruit may not develop properly. If there are more suitable male flowers open, grab them as well and repeat the process on the same female flower. The more the better! That female flower is going to close up tomorrow so you may as well make use of those ready males while they are still around. But also plan ahead. If you see other females that look like they will be ready the next day, save some of the male flowers for later.

If you want to take a more delicate approach you can use a small artist's paint brush to transfer pollen from the male to female flowers. I find this to be overly time-consuming and a little too delicate for smaller flowers. But larger flowers such as pumpkin and squash have giant grains of pollen making it much easier to see and handle on the tip of a brush.

If all goes well you should notice a big change in the female flower ovary within a few days. The stem attaching the ovary to the vine will thicken and elongate and the ovary will start pointing downward. It will start to get larger at a surprising rate as it turns into a melon or cucumber or whatever.

If you have multiple female flowers ready for pollination, do not hesitate to pollinate them. The success rate for this method of pollination is around 50% so do not be overly upset if some of your attempts fail. And if you find yourself with more fruit on your vines than you want, just snip off the weaker ones.

Winter Gardening

Plant hardiness zones are used to describe what types of plants can survive in a given geographical region. The zone designation defines the minimum annual temperature for that particular zone. So when you encounter a plant that is hardy to zone 5a for example, this means it can (in dormancy) survive temperatures as low as -20F (-29C). If you live in zone 5s or higher, there is a good chance this plant can survive through your winter.

You can find plant hardiness zone maps on the internet for the United States at www.planthardiness.ars.usda.gov and for Canada at www.planthardiness.gc.ca

Most of the vegetables and some herbs grown on my balcony are annuals and will not last more than a season regardless of how warm the winters are. But some are perennials that might survive the winter outdoors. Some plants, like parsley and celery are biennials. These are plants that live for two season; growing in the first and producing seeds in the second after a period of dormancy.

But surviving a winter in a container on the balcony is quite different than toughing it out over the winter in an earth-based garden. Unlike being planted in the ground, container-bound plants on the balcony will not enjoy an insulating snow cover or the moisture it brings when temperatures warm up in the spring. The container plant will be at the mercy of cold, drying winds that will quickly rob it of moisture and freeze the soil in which it grows to a solid block of ice.

A plant left out to over-winter on the balcony will need to be protected from the wind. The surface of the container soil should be covered with a mulch to preserve moisture in the potting soil. And it's a good idea to give the container a good drink before the frost comes and again when everything thaws in the spring.

Most of what I grow on my balcony is treated as annuals and I don't bother over-wintering anything out there. The few perennials I've grown that I keep around for another season spend the winter inside in my kitchen window.

There are a number of garden vegetables that can tolerate cooler temperatures and these make good candidates for early spring or fall plantings. Several crops of greens can be started earlier in the spring under cover. By covering newly planted seed and seedlings with a cloche (which is just another word for plant cover) you can protect them from frost. Similarly, if you cover fall crops on nights when you suspect there will be frost, you can protect your plants from frost damage. I've used old bed sheets to temporarily cover some of my containers. Recycled plastic containers and pop bottles also make good covers for smaller plants. I've harvested leafy greens well past my first frost date by simply keeping them covered at night to protect them. When growing under cover outside in cold temperatures these plants will not grow much more but they will stay alive. But eventually, even under cover, the potting soil in these containers will freeze solid, bringing the season to a final close.

Baby greens being kept alive under cover well into December

My Favorite Balcony Vegetables

In the following pages are descriptions of some of the vegetables I have had good luck with on my balcony. When I decide what to grow every year I usually stick to a few crops I know my family will make good use of, such as tomatoes and basil. But I also like to leave some space for growing things I've never grown before. Some plants grow successfully and others fail miserably. When you have such a small space, a single crop usually implies one or two plants growing in a single container. Finding space to take chances and experiment with something new can be tough. Some of the vegetables I've grown successfully on the balcony that are not mentioned here include broccoli, carrots, cucumbers, eggplant, kale, spinach and tomatillos.

Vegetable	Sun	Approx Height	Min Spacing	Container Depth	Starting from
Beans	☼	1 to 6'	4" to 6"	> 8"	Seed or Transplant
Beets	☼ ☽	8 to 12"	3"	>10"	Seed
Cape Gooseberry	☼	4 to 5'	>12"	>12"	Seed or Transplant
Lettuce	☼ ☽	3 to 12"	up to 6"	4 to 8"	Seed or Transplant
Peas	☼ ☽	1 to 6'	2"	8 to 12"	Seed
Peppers	☼	1 to 2'	>6"	8 to 10"	Transplant
Potatoes	☼	4 to 5'	12"	>12"	Seed
Radishes	☼ ☽	6 to 12"	3 to 6"	8"	Seed
Swiss Chard	☼ ☽	1 to 2'	6"	>8"	Seed or Transplant
Tomatoes	☼	1 to 8'	>12"	>12"	Seed or Transplant
Watermelon	☼	> 12'	>12"	>12"	Transplant

Beans

Beans are great plants to start from seed in containers. They grow fast and don't expect much attention. I find you can't go wrong with green or yellow wax bush beans. They are simple to grow, form compact plants, and the whole bean pod is edible. Just give them the basic requirements: sunlight and moisture. Pole beans grow long twisting vines that are great for vertical gardening. But you need to pay a bit more attention to them during the growing season.

Getting Started

Know what you are planting. Not all beans grow into bushes and not all grow edible pods. Bush beans will typically produce a single large crop of beans all at once, whereas pole beans will produce continuously throughout the season. This makes bush beans good candidates for successive plantings. Pole beans will only require a single planting at the beginning of the season.

Like all legumes, beans are able to pull nitrogen available in the atmosphere into their roots for storage. But don't let this stop you from following a regular fertilization routine. After all, plants need more than just nitrogen to grow. In order for nitrogen fixation to take place, a bacteria known as rhizobia needs to be present in the soil. Prior to planting the seeds you can coat them with granulated soil inoculants that contain this bacteria, to give the plants a boost during the growing season.

With the exception of broad beans, beans do not like to be planted in cool soil, so wait until all threat of frost has passed before planting outside. Pole beans are especially sensitive to cooler temperatures and frost.

I always plant my beans directly into the container in which I plan to grow them. You can try to start them indoors and transplant them if you like but they do not transplant well. Given that the seeds are so large and germinate with ease, and that the plants reach maturity in a relatively short amount of time, there really is no need to start them indoors. When planted, the seeds will take about a week to germinate and sprout up through the soil.

Resist the urge to plant them deep. If planted too deep the new leaves can be damaged as the seed sprouts and breaks through the soil surface. Sometimes the new leaves break off entirely. If this happen, be patient. I've had several plants come up like this and they manage to recover.

Growing on the Balcony

All bean varieties have similar water, nutrient and sunlight requirements. They should be grown in full sun with moist soil and good drainage. With the exception of shelling beans, do not leave the pods on the plants to mature. The presence of mature fruit will keep the plants from wanting to produce more.

Bush Beans

Bush beans are some of the simplest vegetable plants you can grow and they do well in containers. When choosing a variety, look for a snap, green or string bean that produces edible pods. Yellow wax beans have similar growing habits to green string beans are another good variety to grow. Just keep in mind that not all bush varieties grow pods that are edible.

Bush bean plants form somewhat compact bushes that grow 1 to 2 feet tall. Space your plants at least 4 inches apart in a container at least 8 inches deep. Bush beans do not like to be crowded. I find that the plants stand up to the wind fairly well but appreciate a bit of support from a stick or two in the soil next to them. Just a little something extra to lean on when they are carrying a heavy load.

Pick new beans before the bean seeds start to bulge inside the pods. This is when they are ready to eat. The sooner you pick them, the sooner the plant will flower and produce the rest of its crop. Young beans are much better tasting. I can get a good handful off of a single plant, which isn't bad considering the minimal space and attention they require. Most bush bean plants do not live long. Depending on the variety they will reach maturity around 55 to 60 days after being planted. Once a plant reaches maturity and has produced a full crop of beans, it is pretty much finished.

Pole Beans

The difference between pole and bush beans is that pole beans only grow if allowed to climb up a pole or other suitable structure. This makes them great for growing when space is limited. Plant with the same spacing and container depth as bush beans: at least 4 inches separation and 8 inches of soil depth. More container space will be appreciated by pole beans. After they grow a few inches tall, they send up a vine that searches for something to wrap itself around. And once they find support, they grow fast.

What you use to support them is your choice. Many gardeners use 3 or 4 poles of 5 or 6 foot length set up like a tepee over a group of 3 or 4 plants. But this tepee approach doesn't work too well on a balcony as it relies on the sunlight passing overhead and shining on all sides of the structure. Since plants on my balcony receive sunlight mainly from one direction, I prefer to use a four foot trellis over a long container and I use lengths of cord or twine tied between the top and bottom horizontal trellis poles for the beans to climb. The vines have no trouble twisting their way up and

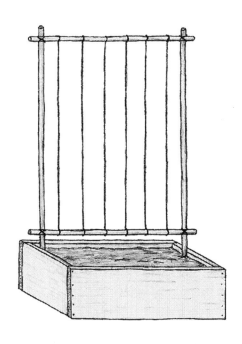

around such a support structure. When the plants reach the top of the support, I just snip off the tops to force branching and growth lower down on the plants. Pole bean vines can reach dizzying heights if you let them, so use whatever size trellis or fence you can manage.

Pole beans take a little longer than bush beans to start producing but when they do, they do so continuously for the remainder of the season. The bean pods tend to be more fibrous than bush varieties but are also more flavorful. Picking them early is necessary to get them while they taste best and to promote further bean production.

Hot windy conditions wreak havoc on my balcony pole beans. During the hottest, sunny days of summer the leaves wilt a little and are easily damaged by any wind that blows and thrashes them about. Spider mites also like to make a mess of my pole beans.

Broad Beans

Broad beans, also known as fava beans, horse beans or pigeon beans, grow like a bush bean but are actually more like a pea plant. They are not all that popular in North American gardens so are not easy to come by. They like cool temperatures and do not do well in the summer heat. But they do alright in containers if given proper sunlight. Just treat them like bush beans and they'll grow fine. Use the same spacing and container depth: at least 4 inches separation and 8 inches of depth. More depth is better. They require about 60 to 65 days to mature.

They are a low-yielding plant so you may need to plant several to get enough beans for a meal. The plants grow up to 2 feet tall with a few stems emanating from the base. The leaves and stems do not resemble those of bush bean plants in any way. The size of the pods produced depends on the variety, but they can contain anywhere from 3 to 6 seeds per pod with the seeds measuring up to an inch in size.

The pods are thick, fibrous, inedible and lined with downy fibers that blanket the meaty bean seeds inside. These seeds are also wrapped in a membrane that some people insist on peeling before eating. If you pick broad beans early enough and peel off this membrane, you will be left with a bean that tastes like a pea. In some cultures it is a culinary faux pas to peel this membrane as it gives the broad bean a richer bean like taste.'

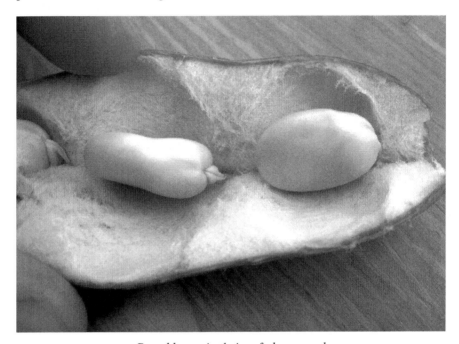

Broad beans in their soft downy pod

Like other beans, pick broad beans when they are young. When the seeds appear to be budging in the pod they are getting closer to maturity. The older the bean, the more bitter it will taste. For fresh eating, pick them when the pods are fat but not bulging.

Shelling Beans

Unlike beans that grow in edible pods, shelling beans are only grown for their edible seed. Some grow as bushes and others as vines requiring support. When growing shelling beans, the pods are left on the plant until they dry out and the seeds bulge inside, indicating the seeds in the pods have matured. You may have to pick a few early to promote further plant growth. As the growing season draws to a close, just leave the beans on the plants until they have withered and died. Popular shelling beans are Kidney, Borlotti, Pinto, Navy, Garbanzo, Lima, Mung and Soybeans.

Shelling beans can be dried and stored for long periods of time, but for a small crop I don't think this effort is justified. You can always buy dried beans, but how often do you find freshly shelled beans for sale? Much better to eat them fresh. They can also be stored for a few months shelled and frozen in the freezer.

Fresh borlotti beans

Shelling beans are best eaten cooked. In fact some beans contain high concentrations of a lectin known as phytohemagglutinin which is a sugar-binding protein that, when ingested, can make you sick. The toxic effects of this lectin can be neutralized by cooking the beans for at least 10 minutes. All beans contain these proteins but most in low concentrations that will not affect most people. Kidney beans are the exception which have the highest concentrations. They should never be eaten raw.

Problems

I have never had much trouble growing beans although I do occasionally have trouble getting them started. It is difficult to get beans to start in overly moist, cool soils. And being an amateur gardener, eager to get things started in the spring, I tend to start the beans a little too early and water them a little too much. Aphids are a minor problem as are spider mites, but with the right growing conditions the plants thrive regardless.

Beets

Beets are good container vegetables that don't require much space to grow. What I really admire about them is that both tops and roots can be eaten at any time during the lifecycle of the plant. Not all beets are red. Golden beets have a sweet taste and their juices do not stain everything they touch. And there are stripped varieties such as Chioggia that look really neat when sliced. Bulls Blood is another variety I've grown, more for its deep red tops than its mediocre root bulb.

Getting Started

Being a root vegetable, they do not transplant well and are one of those vegetables best started from seed in the container in which you plan to grow them. They are a cool weather crop and do not do well during the hot days of summer, so start your seed outside in the spring right around your first frost free date or in the fall, 60 days back from your first frost date.

Beet seeds typically come in a cluster with each cluster containing approximately half a dozen beet seeds. Plant the entire cluster a half inch deep and at least 3 inches from its nearest neighbour. This might seem a little close but beets don't seem to mind. Some varieties can be slow to germinate. As the beet shoots appear, thin them down to a single plant. I prefer to just snip the undesirables with a small pair of scissors, so I

Beet seed clusters

don't disturb the roots of the other nearby tiny beet plants. Beet roots can grow fairly deep so you should give them a container with at least 10 inches of depth. Otherwise they are not overly demanding.

Growing on the Balcony

They grow well in full sun but can tolerate a bit of shade. However being a root vegetable I have found they grow best when the sunlight they receive is from an overhead source. I haven't had much luck getting them started further back under the overhang above my balcony. As the beets grow, hill up potting soil around their exposed shoulders to keep them from turning green and getting tough.

Like other root crops, grow them in a rich potting soil that drains well. Keep them moist or the roots will start to get tough. If it's the tops you are after, use a fertilizer with a good amount of nitrogen in it to promote leafy growth. Otherwise, just use a balanced mix of nutrients. Your goal should be to encourage the beets to grow fast before the warm weather signals them to go to seed.

Harvest

Unless it's just the tops you want, most beet varieties will reach maturity in 50 or 60 days. The root bulbs will form partly above the soil surface, so it's easy to see their progress. However keep in mind that if your potting soil is not terribly rich in nutrients, your containers are shallow or your plants receive less than full sunlight, your beets might not attain a large size. Don't rely entirely on their size to determine maturity. You really don't want to leave them in the ground too long or they will start to develop a tough texture and bitter taste.

Beets are one of those vegetables that can be entirely used in the kitchen at any stage of maturity. Leaves under 5 inches can be harvested as a cut-and-come-again green and used raw in salads. Once the tops get larger they get tougher, but they can still be harvested and boiled or steamed as you would Swiss chard or spinach. The roots can be harvested when they exceed an inch in diameter. The smaller they are the more tender they will be.

Chioggia beets growing in a nice deep container

Cape Gooseberries

The cape gooseberry (*Physalis peruviana*) is a close relative of the ground cherry and the tomatillo. It is not a true gooseberry. The plants grow into large, woody, frost-tender perennial bushes that produce small husk-covered berries with a sweet yet mildly tart taste. They are South American in origin and not South African as many people believe. The "cape" in the name actually refers to the calyx or husk that surrounds the berry while it grows and ripens.

Starting

The plants need 120 to 140 days to produce truly ripe fruit. In Northern regions, to have any chance of getting them to produce fruit, they need to be started indoors in the spring. And they probably shouldn't be transplanted outside until the soil temperature climbs above 68°F (20°C). I've found I can just treat them like tomatoes when it comes to timing seed starting and transplanting.

Finding cape gooseberry seeds might take some effort. There are a few online seed stores that carry them, which is how I get my seed. The seeds are very small and I find them rather difficult to get started. But once they sprout and put out a set of true leaves, I don't usually have any problems with them.

Growing on the Balcony

The plants grow fast once established, quickly reaching 4 or 5 feet in height with a bushy spread. They do well in any container that would be suitable for a medium-size tomato. I've planted pairs of plants in long containers that hold no more than 2 cubic feet of soil with 10 inches of container depth and by the end of the season the container is packed with roots. I'm sure they would do better with more root space. Even so, the plants grow and set fruit. Although they can be grown as perennials in the right climate, most northern gardeners like myself grow them as annuals.

Flower buds will form at the intersections between branches. More branching means more fruit, so force the plant to produce more branches by pinching off the growing tips. They typically start to flower and set fruit after the plant has formed 12 or 13 branch intersections. I also believe that the temperature has to be within an optimal range for the plant to start flowering. And when they do flower, they do so profusely. I've had plants flower and set fruit, stop for a while during the hottest part of summer, then start producing flowers again later in the season.

The plants are not particularly heavy feeders but they do need a good amount of sunlight and moisture to set fruit. I find they can still grow quite large in a partially shady spot and just like tomatoes, their ability to grow tall and spread out gives them an advantage on the balcony. They seem to be able to reach out for the sunlight quite easily.

Cape gooseberries, on the vine and free from the husk

Harvest

It takes a while for the flowers to set fruit and ripen. The flowers are self-pollinating and once pollinated they will point downward, forming what looks like a tiny lantern around a very small green berry. As the berry inside grows, so does the husk around it. It takes a little over a month for the husk to dry out and turn from green to light brown. At the same time the berry inside will begin to ripen from green to yellow. It will take another month for the berry to ripen fully.

Never eat the berries when they are green. Like all members of the nightshade family, all parts of the plant are poisonous to humans except the ripe fruit. The best way to know when the berries are fully ripe is to wait for them to fall from the bush. I seem to wait forever for mine and they never fall so I just pick them when I think they've been on the bush long enough. Not being able to easily peek inside the husk is frustrating but rest assured, as the husk turns yellow and brown, the fruit inside is ripening. Once removed from the plant, the berries can last about a month at room temperature if left inside their husks.

Problems

The branches of these plants are woody and do not flex very much. They are easily snapped off by wind gusts which is a common problem on my balcony. These plants absolutely need some support to keep them from bending too much in the wind. The larger and thicker the branch and the more loaded it is with other branches and leaves, the more likely it is to snap. And I've had branches break off right near the base of the plant, taking half the plant's fruit load with them.

The one insect that has given my cape gooseberry plants the most trouble is the spider mite, but they are fairly easy to deal with and the plants don't seem terribly bothered by them. I have also had problems with nutrient deficiencies late in the season. I always under-estimate how big these plants can get and I usually plant them in containers too small to properly support them. So the nutrient deficiency is no surprise.

Lettuce

Lettuce is suppose to be one of the easiest garden vegetables to grow, yet it's something I've had the most trouble mastering on the balcony. The weather always seems to be too warm or too cold and windy. Over-watering, soil compaction and lack of proper sunlight are constant problems. Sometimes what is easy to grow in the garden is not so easy to grow on the balcony.

Limit your lettuce selection to loose leaf, oak leaf, butterhead and romaine. Loose leaf lettuce is very common and oak is just another leaf lettuce with leaves that look like those of an oak tree. Butterheads are loose-heading varieties and you'll see names like Boston or bib. And of course romaine or cos as it is also known is the ever popular tall and crisp loose-heading variety used in Caesar salads.

Getting Started

Many years ago, I bought a number of small starter lettuce plants at a garden center. It was my first time growing lettuce. I transplanted them into a container and all but one rotted and died. The one that survived grew a couple more inches before we ate it and it didn't taste that great. Since then I have started my own lettuce plants inside in early spring to transplant. When transplanting lettuce you need to ensure it is not planted deeper than it is in its starter container. Do not bury the plant below its crown. If you plant the transplant too deep, the outer leaves will rot. Lately I prefer to direct-seed my lettuce instead of transplanting it.

Lettuce is a cool weather crop and does not appreciate the summer heat. The seeds germinate in soil temperatures as low as 32°F (0°C), so they can be the first thing planted on the balcony in the spring and the last thing planted in the fall as the temperatures start to drop. The seeds will not geminate in temperatures above 85°F (about 30°C). Lettuce has a very shallow root system and does not require much growing depth. This makes it possible to use a wide range of containers for growing lettuce. If you just want small baby greens, 3 or 4 inches of soil depth is enough. For growing plants to maturity, provide 6 or 8 inches.

How you sow the seed depends on how mature you plan to let the plants get before harvesting. For microgreens I just randomly broadcast the seeds over the soil surface, then cover them lightly with more potting soil. The seeds are small and don't have to be planted too deep – no more than 1/4 inch. If growing for baby leaves, you can plant them in a grid pattern an inch or two apart. To grow full size plants they should be seeded 4 to 6 inches apart. Another approach is to seed densely, perhaps by broadcasting, and as the plants grow and crowd one another, thin them out. Use what you pull up as you thin them over time. When you get down to one plant per half square foot, let them grow to maturity.

Growing on the Balcony

Lettuce should be grown in a rich fertile soil. Use lots of compost as the organic mater will contain lots of nutrients and it will help to retain moisture. It is important to get your lettuce growing fast so it can be harvested before the weather gets too warm. Providing the plants with all the nutrients they want and need is the best way to do this. Since the leaves are the only thing to harvest, use a fertilizer that is higher in nitrogen to give them a boost.

Lettuce plants have a high moisture content and you need to keep them well-watered. Drip irrigation or a small self-watering container will work best. But, as always, be careful not to over-water the plants.

The biggest problem I have with lettuce is providing the right amount of sunlight. Being a plant that grows close to the ground, lettuce responds best to overhead sunlight. I find that when it receives all of its sunlight from an angle, it tends to grow tall and leggy as if trying to angle itself towards the sunlight. For this reason I place my lettuce at the edge of my balcony where it can catch as much overhead sunlight as possible.

All that sunlight can also overheat the plants so keep the containers in a spot where the sun does not fall directly on the container. A little bit of dappled shade during the hottest part of

Bolting romaine lettuce

the day will help to keep the plants cool. Lettuce thrives in temperatures below 70°F (21°C). When it reaches maturity and the weather is hot, or the plant experiences stress, it will start to bolt; the center of the plant will grow really tall into a stalk with flowers at the top. If this starts to happen, all hope of harvesting tender tasty lettuce leaves is lost.

Black Seeded Simpson

Harvest

Lettuce will reach maturity anywhere from 40 to 60 days after germination depending on the variety. I find the best time to eat lettuce is when it is young. Baby greens make wonderful salads. It doesn't take long to get lettuce plants to grow to a size appropriate for baby leaf harvesting. You can start harvesting as early as a couple of weeks after the plants break the soil surface. The great thing is that you can cut a few outer leaves and leave the younger inner leaves to grow a little more for the next round of salads. This harvesting method is called cut-and-come-again and the trick is simply to leave the young inner leaves around the heart of the plant so they can continue to develop. Just remember to always harvest early in the day before it gets too hot outside as lettuce leaves wilt in the heat and are easily damaged.

Problems

Most of my problems with lettuce result from unfriendly environmental conditions. I've seen a few aphids sucking on my lettuce plants from time to time but they don't seem to thrive there. I've over-watered lettuce in the past and watched it rot. If it looks droopy in the late afternoon heat, that's understandable. But if it looks that way in the morning, you have a problem. Avoid bitter tasting leaves by keeping it properly watered. It doesn't take much stress for lettuce to start tasting bitter.

Peas

Fresh peas rarely make it off my balcony. As soon as I see a pod ready to pick, I do so and eat it right there on the balcony! I never seem to have more than a couple to eat at a time. For me there is nothing better than freshly picked garden peas.

With peas, you have three main varieties to consider: shelling, snow and snap (or sugar). Snow and snap peas grow pods that are edible and shelling peas do not. Snap peas are my favorite and are currently the only peas I bother to grow. They have nice thick pods with a crunchy refreshing taste. Some peas grow into long climbing vines and others grow shorter, bushier plants.

Getting Started.

Seed peas directly into the container in which you plan to grow them. They germinate best when the soil temperature is above 50°F (10°C). In the early spring, garden soils are typically cool and damp and this combination can create problems for germinating seeds. If the soil is too moist, the new seed will rot or fall prey to fungal infection. But in a container garden the soils tends to be warmer and you control the moisture, so you should have an easier time getting your seeds to sprout. Some seed will come with a fungicide pre-applied to help combat the problems associated with starting the seeds in the cool dampness of spring.

Sow pea seeds no more than an inch deep. You can plant them fairly close together; a couple of inches apart. With more space between the plants you should get a slightly higher yield per plant, but with more plants in the container you'll get a greater yield overall. Each pea plant will only give you a few pods so don't be afraid to plant lots. Growing them close together also means they can rely on each other somewhat for support. Ideally you will already have something in mind for supporting your crop so plant the seeds where they can make the best use of your planned support structure.

Peas have a deep growing tap root so try to give your peas at least 12 inches of container depth. I've grown them in containers as little as 8 inches deep and they grow alright but they don't get very tall and they don't produce a whole lot of peas.

Growing on the Balcony

Like all cool weather crops, give peas rich potting soil and keep the nutrients flowing. They grow best when temperatures are below 70°F (21°C) so you need the plants to grow fast to take advantage of the cool weather. The plants are susceptible to mildew so try to avoid watering the leaves. I find they are also somewhat popular with the spider mites.

Snap peas

Regardless of variety, bush or vine, the plants grow with tendrils that reach out and wrap themselves around anything they can find. Their growing habits vary somewhat but bush varieties grown in containers will grow between 1 and 2 feet in height, whereas vine varieties can grow 6 feet or more. And despite some varieties being labeled as bush or dwarf peas, they all grow much better if you provide them with something to climb and cling to.

If you are growing a tall vining variety, you will need a trellis for the peas to climb. A trellis similar to one required for growing pole beans (page 80) would work just fine. For shorter bush varieties, some gardeners just poke some sticks in the ground parallel to the row of peas. If you plant the peas dense enough, they should be able to use the sticks and each other for support. I've tried this and found the peas had problems maintaining a grasp on the sticks and each other when it got too windy. They actually have a better time when planted next to another stronger plant they can use for support. Nylon netting is available to let you create a little temporary trellis for the peas to climb, but I find it to be a bit of a pain to set-up as it requires something sturdy to support it. A tomato cage could also be used. Put the cage over a dense planting of peas so they grow up into the cage. However the frame of the tomato cage might not offer enough support structure for all of the peas to grab on to.

I've used a heavy plastic mesh held up like a fence beside a row of peas. If the openings in the mesh are small enough, the peas will have no problem finding something to hold on to. You could also use chicken wire as it will pretty much stand on its own. Plant a container with lots of pea plants and then shape the chicken wire to stand around the inside edge of the container to act as a fence. The peas will cling to the chicken wire fence and each other.

Being nitrogen fixers like beans and other legumes, if enough rhizobia bacteria is available in the soil the plants should be able to pull enough atmospheric nitrogen into their roots to satisfy their needs (page 79). But peas use up a lot of nitrogen and do better when given more. They require a balance of nutrients just like other vegetables so fertilize them as you would any other vegetable growing on your balcony.

Harvest

Peas reach maturity in about 60 days. The flowers are self-pollinating and do not require any outside assistance to get the job done. To keep the plants producing you should pick mature pods as soon as you can. Snap peas are best picked when the seeds start to bulge in the pod. Shelling peas should be picked well in advance of this stage. The sooner the better, although waiting will give you bigger peas. Snow peas should be picked as soon as you notice the seeds developing inside the pod.

Peppers

In the springtime, pepper plants are nearly as popular as tomatoes at the garden centers in my city. They are surprisingly easy to grow and rather compact in size. They don't sprawl all over the place and you don't need a massive container the size of a bath tub to keep them happy which makes them great balcony container plants.

There are so many different varieties of pepper to choose from with different shapes, colours and sizes. Some are sweet and others spicy. California Wonder, Cubanelle, Jalapeño, Hungarian Hot Wax and Klari Baby Cheese are a few that I've had good luck with.

Hungarian Hot Wax Peppers

Getting Started

Unless you live in a warmer climate, peppers are best started early indoors. They do not tolerate cool temperatures. If you start from seed indoors, start them a couple of months before the date you plan to set them out. I like to transplant mine between the end of May and beginning of June so I start my seeds inside between the end of March and early April. When growing indoors, watch for yellow, curling or falling leaves. This is a sign that the tiny plants need some nourishment. It can also be a sign of over-watering.

You can purchase starter plants from a garden center in the spring but try to stay away from plants that are already flowering or have set fruit. When you transplant these plants the flowers might set fruit and the fruit might develop to maturity, however the overall plant yield will be lower. I prefer my starter plants to start life after transplant growing new roots and stems so they can support more fruit. If the plant is already fruiting, it is less likely to devote energy to growing more infrastructure.

Plant your pepper plants outside when the nighttime temperatures are consistently above 60°F (15°C). Peppers do not like cold soil. If you want to try for an earlier outside date, you can always watch the forecast and bring your plants inside when you sense that the temperatures will fall below 50°F (10°C).

Peppers do not have large root systems and when grown in containers the plants typically grow to about 1 or 2 feet in height with a spread of 1 foot. A standard 1 or 2 gallon container should be sufficient for some of the smaller varieties. I have some rectangular planters 24 x 12 inches and 10 inches deep and I find these easily support a pair of pepper plants.

Growing Requirements

Peppers tend to be a little more fussy about sunlight than their tomato cousins. Because they grow into somewhat stocky and compact plants, they do not climb and collect sunlight like a plant with vining habits. You have to be a little more selective when it comes to placing them on your balcony. Peppers will refuse to flower or set fruit without adequate sunlight.

They enjoy consistently moist soil and they will benefit from a self-watering container or drip irrigation system. They like to have a constant supply of moisture and nutrients but don't like having soaking wet roots.

When planting peppers it is not necessary to provide them with support but if they are exposed to lots of wind, as mine usually are, provide a stick or two next to each plant to give them something to lean on when the wind starts to blow. Tomato cages are also a good way to provide support, although I find the plants sustain a fair bit of damage when the winds thrash them against the inside of the tomato cage.

Pepper plants form perfect flowers that have both male and female parts so pollinating is not a problem. The optimal temperature range for flowering and fruit set is 60°F to 75°F (15°C to 24°C). Temperatures above or below this range may cause the plant to drop blossoms. The flower pollen becomes sterile at temperatures above 90°F (32°C).[*] For these reasons, you may find that a plant that is producing lots of flowers and setting fruit suddenly stops doing so in the middle of the summer. As the cooler temperatures return, the plant will likely start flowering and producing fruit again.

I find it difficult to grow a good sweet pepper on my balcony. If the plants are stressed with infrequent watering, lack of sunlight or a nutrient deficiency, the peppers do not turn out as sweet as I like. But hot peppers are a little more forgiving. Hot pepper plants desire similar growing conditions but unlike sweet peppers, a little bitterness and toughness can usually be overlooked. My hot peppers end up sliced on a pizza, simmered down into a sauce or blended into a chutney. So unlike the sweet peppers that I like to eat fresh and raw, I can somewhat neglect and abuse the hot peppers and still end up with a usable crop.

Harvest

Did you know that red bell peppers are just ripe green peppers? Peppers will ripen to yellow, red, orange or purple depending on the variety. Green peppers are typically more bitter than ripe peppers but also more crisp. Even jalapeño peppers will ripen to a bright red if left on the plant long enough, but they are typically picked while still green. There is no single best time to pick a pepper. It all depends on the variety and your taste.

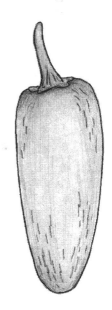

Hot peppers will be hotter if left to mature, but will be more crisp if picked early. Some hot peppers show maturity with small lines that appear along their bodies. This is known as corking and is common on ripe Jalapeño peppers. The appearance of these lines is usually a good indication that a pepper is ready to be picked. Most pepper varieties will take over 100 days to reach maturity from seed.

Corking lines on a Jalapeño Pepper

---

[*] The Effect of Extreme Temperatures on the Tomato and Pepper Crop. Ontario Ministry of Agricultural, Food and Rural Affairs.

http://www.omafra.gov.on.ca/english/crops/facts/info_tomtemp.htm

When picking peppers, like any fruiting vegetable, be careful not to break the plant stems. Use scissors or shears to clip larger peppers from their plants and leave a good bit of the stem on the pepper (they'll keep longer this way). And be extra careful when picking hot peppers, particularly the super spicy kind such as Habaneros. Getting even a little bit of the juice on your hands will cause you lots of grief if you happen to wipe your eyes or other sensitive areas of your body. When picking and handling these super hot peppers, consider wearing gloves.

Pepper Heat

Capsaicin is the chemical compound that makes peppers hot. It is highly concentrated in the white membrane in the pepper that holds the seeds, not in the seeds themselves as some people believe. All peppers contain this compound to a varying degree except bell peppers. When capsaicin comes in contact with human skin it tends to cause a burning sensation. Since it does not dissolve or break down, the sensation remains until it is flushed away.

Hot pepper heat is measured on the Scoville Scale with the unit of measure being the Scoville Heat Unit or SHU. It indicates the relative amount of dilution necessary to make the heat from a pepper barely detectable by a panel of judges. Bell peppers have a rating of 0 where as Jalapeños have a rating of 2500-5000. Habaneros measure between 100,000 and 300,000. And Bhut Jolokias have been tested as high as 1 million. But keep in mind that the scale is highly subjective. Growing conditions can have a big impact on capsaicin levels.

Problems

Aphids are always a problem for me when I grow peppers. I have yet to find a way to control them but keeping my plants healthy and squishing or spraying the aphids off the plants from time to time helps.

Peppers are also susceptible to sun scalding. The fruit should be shaded from excessive direct sunlight or the skin of the fruit will burn. Blossom end rot is another problem which results in the lower end of the fruit rotting while it is still on the plant. Lack of calcium will result in blossom end rot, as will improper watering.

I've had plants abort their leaves after the leaves turned yellow and wilted and this sometimes happens to me during the hottest part of the summer when I have a tendency to over-water everything. Under-watering and over-fertilization can lead to leaf loss and blossom drop.

Potatoes

I think growing potatoes in containers is an interesting challenge. There is a trick to it but it's not difficult to do. The advantage of growing your own potatoes is that you will have access to the freshest new potatoes you can get your hands on. New potatoes are not a variety of potato but simply immature potatoes, dug up before all of their sugars convert to starches and before their delicate skins turn thick and rough.

There are too many potato varieties to mention and none that I am terribly familiar with. For container growing you should use an early variety. There are three main categories of potato: First Early, Second Early and Maincrop. The difference between these categories is the amount of time it takes for the plants to grow and produce a crop of mature potato tubers. First Early potatoes will be ready in 8 to 12 weeks depending on the specific variety. And more importantly, they result in more compact plants with smaller tubers. These first early potatoes are also known as salad potatoes and they are your best bet for growing potatoes on the balcony.

Getting Started

The easiest way to grow potatoes is to start with a seed potato. Potato plants do set fruit and form seeds, but it is more common and much easier to grow new plants from existing tubers. A potato tuber planted in the ground will send out new shoots and roots on which new tubers will form. If you just want to experiment with potato growing in containers, I recommend starting with an organic store-bought potato. Perhaps you already have one lurking in the back of a dark cupboard, neglected and lonely. Just be sure to use an organically grown potato so you know it is free of chemical contamination.

But if you want to get serious about growing them, you should source some seed potatoes. Seed potatoes are just small potatoes ideally suited for seeding new plants. They are grown under ideal conditions to be disease free and provide the best chance for a good crop.

The potato you choose for seed will need to be prepared before planting. They should not be too old or already sprouting like mad. You want to start with a tuber that is firm, healthy and still full of energy. Ensure that your seed potato has at least one eye on it and preferably no more than three. The eye is a bud and is what forms the stalk of the plant. Some people recommend chitting seed potato before planting. This means simply placing them somewhere in the dark to get them to start sprouting. The seed tubers are ready to plant when the shoots grow to about a half inch in length. If your seed tuber has too many eyes and results in more than three sprouts, just rub off the extras before planting and be sure the ones you keep are all on the same side. If you are starting with a potato that was already festering away in the dark someplace, chances are it is already well on its way to growing with no chitting necessary.

Although I've never tried it this way, you can also start with a larger seed potato cut into smaller chunks. You just need to ensure there are a few eyes on each chunk. After cutting the potato, let the pieces sit for a while before planting them so the cut edges can dry out and cure.

Growing on the Balcony

Potatoes like a rich soil with good drainage. The richer the better, so add lots of compost but use a soil mix that drains well. They also thrive in soil that is slightly more acidic than that favored by other garden vegetables but don't be overly concerned with this. You need to keep the potting soil moist but like other root vegetables, over-watering risks rotting the tubers, particularly during the cooler part of the season. This is where a self-watering container works wonders by keeping the plant constantly hydrated without drowning it.

Half full and ready for more potting soil

Choose a large deep container to obtain large yields. A 5 gallon bucket is a popular container for potato growing. With something the size of a storage tote you can easily grow 2 or 3 plants. Overcrowding the container will only result in smaller and/or fewer potatoes. Plant the seed potato deep to increase the size of your harvest. Fill the container with 1/3 potting soil and plant your seed potatoes an inch or two into the soil with the sprouted eyes pointing up. As the plants grow, continue to add soil, leaving the top few inches of the plant exposed. New lateral shoots known as stolons will form along the stem that has been buried. By maximizing the number of stolons on your plant you potentially increase the size of your harvest because potato tubers form at the end of the stolons.

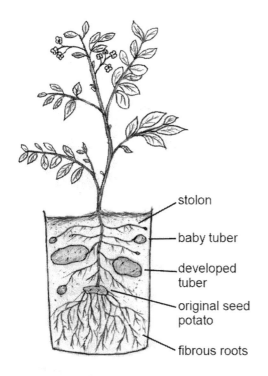

Potatoes are a cool weather crop and do not do well in the summer heat. The tubers develop best when temperatures are between 60°F and 68°F (15°C and 20°C). When temperatures rise above 86°F (30°C) tuber development slows to a halt[*].

Potato plants grow fast and will eventually flower. Don't be too concerned about the flowers. Sometimes they even set fruit but do not eat these little green potato fruit as they will make you ill. Give the plant as much sunlight as you can. Just because the potatoes are beneath the soil does not mean the plant requires less light. But do not expose the growing potato tubers to sunlight. Make sure they stay well buried. Exposed potatoes will develop chlorophyll and also a mildly toxic compound known as solanine. The chlorophyll will turn the potatoes green and as a general rule, potatoes that are green with chlorophyll are likely to also contain lots of solanine, which if eaten can make you sick. Do not eat green potatoes.

---

* Commercial Potato Production - Botany of the Potato Plant. Manitoba Agriculture, Food and Rural Initiatives.

https://www.gov.mb.ca/agriculture/crops/potatoes/bda04s02.html

Harvest

A flowering potato plant usually indicates the beginning of the phase during which the plant produces tubers. This phase of tuber growth will end when the leaves and vines start to yellow and wither. Harvesting the entire container too early will only result in lots of really tiny potatoes. You can reach in and start pulling tubers out of the soil at any time after flowering is underway. Or just feel around to check on their progress. The potatoes you harvest will taste different as the plant ages and early new potatoes are the tastiest. There are special containers available just for growing potatoes, that have doors in the sides to provide access to the crop without disturbing the plant.

Eventually the entire top of the plant will wither and die off. Leaving potatoes in the container after this point will not result in any new growth. So at this time, chop off the top of the plant and empty the contents of the container onto a ground sheet or into a tote. Dig through the soil and roots to harvest your potatoes.

Problems

I have found aphids on my potatoes but they don't appear to thrive there. And being on a balcony means you shouldn't need to worry about burrowing animals nibbling your crop. And you also don't need to worry about pollination. Providing the required nutrients and the right balance of moisture are the bigest challenges and if you can get this right, there isn't much else that can go wrong.

Potato blight is a disease caused by the a fungus known as Phytophthora infestans. The spores of this fungus are easily spread by the wind and result in some serious damage to potato crops. Plants affected by blight exhibit dark brown leaf and stem patches that spread until the plant dies. Infected tubers will rot. If caught early, infected plant matter or even the entire above ground part of the plant, can be removed and disposed of before the blight spreads to the tubers. Early potato varieties are particularly susceptible to blight but being early varieties, they are usually grown and harvested before blight gets around to affecting them.

Radishes

Small early season radishes are the easiest to grow. Cherry Belle is a typical North American garden radish that I grow often: small, round, and red skinned with a white interior. It requires about 28 days to reach maturity. French Breakfast are also popular on my balcony. They grow with an elongated root that has a rounded white bottom.

Some radishes require a longer growing season but can reach a larger size. These larger radishes are best grown in the fall. Black Spanish radishes take about 60 days to mature. These are beastly radishes that can grow quite large. Beneath their tough dark skin is a bright white flesh that has a lot of character.

My favorite late season radish is the Watermelon radish. They grow to the size and shape of an egg with white or light green skin and a bright red interior. They look beautiful when sliced and have a nice mild radish taste.

Getting Started

Early season radishes with short growing times can be planted anytime during the growing season. However they prefer cooler temperatures and will do best when planted in the spring or fall. Radishes that require a longer growing season are best planted when they can take their time maturing in the cooler temperatures, so plant those radishes in the fall, 60 days back form your first frost date. You can also start them in the spring but there is a chance they won't reach maturity before the summer sun coaxes them into going to seed.

Do not bother attempting to transplant radishes. They don't transplant well and it is simply not worth the effort. Start them from seed outdoors when the temperatures climb above 60°F (15°C). The smaller radishes can be grown in containers as little as 6 inches deep but larger radishes should be in containers with at least 8 inches of depth. The seeds are fairly large so plant them 1/4 to 1/2 inch deep and at least 3 inches apart. Leave 6 inches between larger varieties.

Growing on the Balcony

There really isn't much that can go wrong with radishes. To grow really good radishes, you need to grow them quickly. Use a nice fertile potting soil. Radishes grown in warmer temperatures tend to develop a pithy texture and overly hot taste. They also go to seed faster when the weather gets warm. Radishes that have started producing seed will not taste as good. Keep your radishes well-watered and they will taste much better. A self-watering container should work nicely although I've never grown them in one myself. They will grow in partial sun but I find they do best under overhead sunlight. When they don't receive enough sunlight, they tend to grow long and leggy and this is not a good thing for a root vegetable.

Harvest

Some varieties can reach maturity in as little as four weeks. How big your radishes grow depends a lot on their growing conditions. If your radishes don't seem to grow as big as you think they should, resist the temptation to leave them in the ground to keep growing. Pull them up and enjoy them before they get too old and take on a woody taste.

The biggest problem I have with radishes is knowing what to do with them. It's too easy to grow more than I can eat.

Watermelon radish

Swiss Chard

Chard or Swiss chard is related to the garden beet but grows as a tall leafy green on thick stalks over a foot tall. Some people treat it as a substitute for spinach, to be boiled or steamed. Swiss chard is also grown for its ornamental qualities. Fordhook giant is a popular variety that grows large dark green leaves on thick white stalks. Bright lights is a little less productive but with stalks of red, orange, violet and yellow, it makes for a much more decorative container.

Getting Started

Even though it's known for being a cold-tolerant crop, Swiss chard can also tolerate a bit of summer heat. More so than spinach. I have started Swiss chard indoors and transplanted it out a few weeks later but it's relatively easy to grow from seed and will be just fine if you start it outside also. Plant outside as early as a couple of weeks before your last frost date or count back 60 days from your first frost date for a fall crop.

Use a container that has at least 8 inches of depth if you want to grow chard to maturity. Some varieties can grow quite large, so use a deeper container for those. Like its bulb-forming cousin, the beet, it likes to send its roots deep. And just like beets, Swiss chard seeds come in clusters that will grow about a half dozen seedlings. Plant the entire cluster a half inch deep and 6 inches from its nearest neighbour. Give more space for larger varieties. As the tiny chard seedlings appear, thin them down to a single plant. I like to use a pair of scissors to trim away the seedlings I don't want, to avoid disturbing the ones I want to keep.

Growing on the Balcony

Swiss chard is very easy to grow and makes an excellent balcony container plant. It doesn't have many enemies and on my balcony I have yet to see it play host to insects or mold.

I like to start my chard with a good amount of overhead sunlight, but once it starts to reach maturity I find it does just as well in partial shade. Swiss chard isn't overly fussy about its soil conditions, but keep its soil moist and don't let it dry out or the leaves may develop a bitter taste. It doesn't have any special nutrient needs. Swiss chard is a cold-tolerant plant and can handle a frost or two. Even if frost damages the outer leaves of the plant, the inner leaves may still survive.

Swiss chard is a biennial and likes to bolt and produce seed in its second year of growth. But in a typical garden, particularly on the balcony, it's grown as an annual. You would think this means you'll never see it bolt, but apparently fluctuation in temperature and water supply can trick Swiss chard into bolting early. I've never had this happen to my Swiss chard but I hear it's a sight to behold. And apparently, the leaves will retain their taste after bolting so unlike lettuce, all is not lost.

Harvest

Swiss chard can take up to 60 days to reach maturity, but you can start harvesting leaves as soon as they reach a few inches in height. Young tender leaves can be eaten raw in salads with other greens. If you only harvest the outer leaves of the plant, the inner leaves will continue to grow for cut-and-come-again harvesting. When the plant is mature, these young inner leaves will be the most tender.

Swiss chard

Tomatoes

Tomatoes have to be one of the most rewarding vegetables to grow and definitely one of my favorites. They come in all shapes, sizes and colours and entire books have been written describing the various varieties. From tiny pea sized currant tomatoes to massive juicy beefsteaks. From perfectly round to down right ugly!

My favorite tomatoes are large heirloom beefsteak tomatoes. The bigger the better. These are huge meaty tomatoes with few seeds, dense flesh and a wonderful rich tomato taste. But these large tomatoes grow on vines that can reach 7 or 8 feet in height. Growing them on a balcony can take a bit of effort.

Smaller cherry tomatoes are always popular with my family too and I've had good results with Sungold, Sweet 100 and Black Cherry tomatoes. But don't let the size of the fruit fool you. Small tomatoes don't necessarily grow on small plants.

Determinate versus Indeterminate

Tomato growing habits are categorized in one of two ways: determinate or indeterminate. The most suitable tomatoes for container gardening are determinates but I rarely grow them. Determinate varieties produce a set number of fruit all at about the same time before the plant dies off for good. Indeterminate varieties do not stop growing and produce tomatoes all season long. The growth of determinate tomato plants is much more controlled and predictable and for this reason they should be more suitable for container growing. However, that doesn't mean you should rule out indeterminate varieties.

The long vining habits of indeterminate tomato plants can be an advantage to balcony gardeners as the vines can be staked or trellised to catch sunlight from the side if it is not available from an overhead source. This is the case with tomatoes on my balcony. I grow very tall tomato plants, letting them stretch out to catch the afternoon sun. But these large plants require lots of nutrients, moisture and support.

Getting Started

It is easy to find seedlings at garden centers in the spring and if you are new to growing tomatoes, this is how I suggest you start. When buying baby tomato plants, stay away from plants that are already flowering or fruiting. Look for stocky, healthy plants instead. It will likely be too cold outside for plants with early flowers to set fruit and besides, a newly transplanted tomato should spend its early days growing new roots and vines, not producing fruit. A large, healthy plant will produce far more fruit than a small, scrawny one that flowers early.

A pair of 7 foot tomato plants in a single self-watering container

I like to grow my tomatoes from seed because there are many more varieties available to me this way. The garden centers I frequent do not carry many different tomato varieties. And most of them have very vague labeling. I never really know what they're trying to sell me. If your growing season is long enough, you could seed the tomatoes outside directly into the container in which you plan to grow them. However to get an early and more controlled start to the season, you should start them in small 4 inch pots indoors in a sunny window or under a growlight. Plant the seeds 1/4 to 1/2 inch deep and keep them moist.

Tomatoes develop very large root systems that will quickly grow to fill whatever container you plant them in. If you don't have space for large containers, consider growing smaller varieties suited for container growing. Determinate cherry tomatoes that form bushy plants are a good choice, as are tumbler varieties which are hybrids suitable for hanging baskets. Always research whatever variety you plan to grow and be sure you have the resources to grow it. I've grown large Brandywine tomatoes with 8 foot vines in 15 inch wide, 12 inch deep containers. For much of the summer I had to water them twice a day and add fertilizer every other day. They grew large but didn't produce very many tomatoes. For a large indeterminate tomato plant, even a 5 gallon bucket would be a tight fit for a single plant. But it would be a great size for a smaller determinate tomato plant.

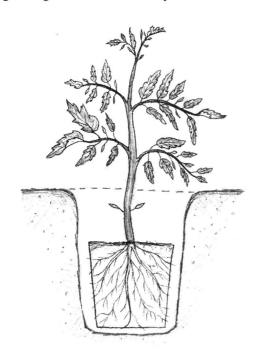

Plant tomatoes deep to encourage root formation

Acclimatize your tomato seedlings in preparation for transplanting. You can start transplanting when the soil temperature reaches 65°F (18°C). When transplanting tomato seedlings, set them into the soil deeper than the first set of leaves on the plant. New roots will form all along the part of the plant stem that is buried. Fill the hole with potting soil and give the plant a good drink. And like all container vegetables, be sure to use a nice rich potting soil that drains well.

Growing on the Balcony

Tomatoes are extremely thirsty plants. They transpire profusely and need to be watered regularly. Avoid periods of drought followed by over-watering. If you fail to water your tomatoes in a timely manner, the fruit on the plant will suffer. Ideally what you want to do is to keep the plant well watered until it has set fruit and then ease off on the watering a bit. Ripening tomatoes that experience periods of drought followed by over-watering will develop thick skins and deep cracks. A self-watering container will do a nice job of balancing the water cycle, giving the plant all the water it needs when it needs it.

Tomatoes are self-pollinating with perfect flowers: the flowers contain both male and female parts. They release pollen when it is warm and dry during the day with temperatures optimally between 65 and 80°F (18.5 to 27.5°C). *Above and below this range there is less chance the flowers will set fruit. If you grow your plants in an area sheltered from the wind, you might need to ensure they get a good shake during the day to assist with pollination.

Being heavy feeders, container grown tomatoes are prone to suffer from a number of nutrient deficiencies. Keep an eye out for yellowing leaves, brown or purple spots and curled leaves. You can provide your tomatoes with a well-balanced general purpose fertilizer all season or use one with a higher nitrogen content during early growth stages, then switch to one with less nitrogen when the plant starts to flower. Another nutrient tomatoes crave is calcium. Calcium deficiencies can lead to blossom end rot.

Tomato plants enjoy the heat of summer but when temperatures rise too high they slow down and even stop setting fruit. This is one reason to start tomatoes early; to get a round of fruit growing on the vines before summer temperatures peak. Once the temperatures start to fall, tomatoes will start setting fruit again. Sometimes I find this comes too late in the season and I'm left with a lot of unripened tomatoes on my vines by late fall.

Supporting Tomato Plants

The first time I grew Brandywine tomatoes I used short-wire tomato cages to give the plants some support. The plants quickly grew up over the tops

---

* The Effect of Extreme Temperatures on the Tomato and Pepper Crop. Ontario Ministry of Agricultural, Food and Rural Affairs.

http://www.omafra.gov.on.ca/english/crops/facts/info_tomtemp.htm

of their cages and eventually collapsed under their own weight, sprawling out along the floor of my balcony and everything else they were next to. Smaller tomato cages are great for short plants like bushy determinates, but for large indeterminates I find them rather useless. And when I do make use of them I find the constant thrashing my plants get from the turbulent balcony wind rubs the plants up against the cages, damaging the leaves and vines.

In a garden, staking indeterminate tomatoes is a popular way to support them and you can do this in a container also. However on a balcony you will need to add some additional support as there will not be enough depth in your container to drive a single stake down far enough. When your

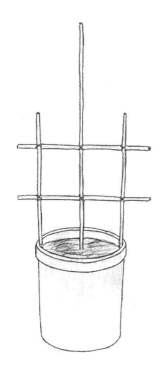

tomato plants are young and no more than a couple of feet tall, or when you first transplant them, drive a pole into the container a few inches away from them. Then gently tie the main vine to the pole with twine, ribbon, an old sock… whatever works. Just don't tie it too tight as you do not want to choke and damage the vine. I also like to add additional poles driven into the container around the edge for added support. If you use bamboo, you can weave a few horizontal poles between the upright stakes to create a sort of trellis. A trellis is a good way to support a tomato growing on a balcony because it lets you fan the vines out against the structure to maximize sunlight exposure.

You can buy stakes specifically for tomato growing at any garden center. These are typically wood and 3/4 or 1 inch square. Plastic coated metal poles are another option. I've been using six foot bamboo poles for some time now. When the plants grow taller than my poles I just get some twine and masking tape and attach new poles to the existing ones. It's not pretty but it works.

When a cluster of tomatoes forms on your plant, consider tying up the vine close to the cluster to take some of the weight off the vine. This is especially true for really large and heavy tomatoes.

When using something smooth for a stake, like bamboo, be sure the plant is secure from buckling at its base. I've had cases where the weight of the plant causes it to buckle near the soil surface, allowing the plant to slide down the stake under its own weight. More friction between the stake and bindings would have prevented this.

Pruning Tomato Plants

Do not prune determinate tomato plants. They don't need it. When staking an indeterminate tomato plant, the goal is to limit its growth to a single main vine. You do this by pruning off new branches as they fork out from the main one. More growth means more leaves, but all those leaves cast shadows on lower leaves and the extra growth uses up precious nutrients without offering much in return. But you don't want to prune off too much. Not enough plant growth will result in lower tomato yield and quality.

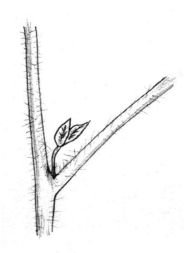

Knowing what to prune can take some practice. Sometimes knowing which vine is the central vine is not always obvious. I usually stake my tomatoes and try to restrict them to one central vine. However I tend to get lazy and end up with a few large branches as the season progresses. When my plants get too large and unmanageable, I just prune some of the growth or pinch off the tips to keep branches from growing further.

A sucker forming between two branches

Once you are comfortable with growing and staking tomatoes you'll find you can be quite aggressive with pruning.

Suckers are new growth that forms at the joint or crotch between two branches on indeterminate plants. There is no harm in leaving them on the plant to grow. But the plant can only draw so much nutrient up from its roots and any fruit that forms on the sucker might not get what it needs to fully grow. I end up keeping a few on my plants, usually because I don't always notice them. Small suckers can be pinched off the plant. Sometimes they just snap off. Or just pinch off the growing tips to keep them from growing longer.

Harvest

Obviously a tomato that changes from green to red is ripe and even green tomato varieties will change colour somewhat as they ripen. But the best way to judge ripeness is by feeling the tomato for firmness. It should have some give and feel easy to crush. An unripe tomato will feel hard like an apple. Time to maturity varies greatly between tomato varieties. Some smaller 'cool' weather hybrids can be ready in as little as 50 days from transplant where as some of the larger heirloom types can take up to 80 days to produce a juicy ripe tomato.

When picking tomatoes I find it best to clip them off the vine with shears or scissors, leaving some of the vine still attached to the fruit. There is less risk of damage to the plant and the tomato this way.

Over ripe tomatoes may split a little when picked. I've found this to be a big problem with cherry tomatoes, even when I leave a bit of the stem attached. Sometimes fully ripe cherry tomatoes will bulge on the vines so much that the slightest disturbance or shock will cause them to erupt. I like to pick these tomatoes before they fully ripen and then let them ripen for a few days indoors before eating them.

You can pick unripe tomatoes and let them ripen on their own by simply placing them somewhere out of the sunlight and letting them sit. Do not place them on a window sill. And do not store them in the refrigerator. Refrigeration will ruin the flavor. Tomatoes that are very unripe will eventually ripen but by that time they will have started to lose moisture and shrivel up.

Problems

The only pests I've seen taking advantage of my balcony tomato plants are whiteflies but they have never created any real problems for me. I have never seen aphids on my tomatoes. And even spider mites seem to stay away. A popular tomato pest is the tomato hornworm: a big ugly green caterpillar that devours tomato plants. Fortunately I've never seen one on my balcony.

Other than some serious nutrient deficiencies and powdery mildew late in the season, most of the problems I have with tomatoes are with the fruit itself. Cat facing is a common problem with heirloom tomatoes. Tomatoes that are cat-faced have folds and scars on their bottoms. There is nothing really wrong with a tomato like this and I just cut around the tough inedible

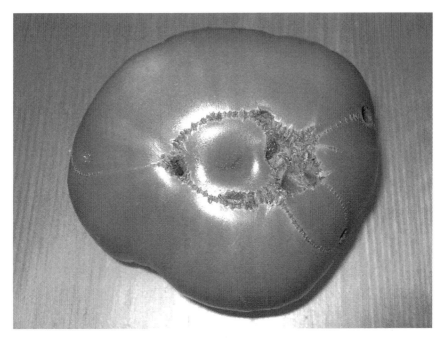

Minor amount of catfacing

Blossom end rot

bits. Cat facing can occur when temperatures drop below 55°F (13°C) during flower production.[*]

One year I grew Opalka tomatoes and over half of the fruit suffered from blossom end rot. This can be caused by a calcium deficiency or over-watering. But some tomato varieties, like Opalka, are more susceptible to end rot than others. A tomato with end rot will form a black moldy spot that starts to rot the bottom end of the tomato. I just pull these from the vine and toss them away.

Another fairly common problem with tomatoes is sun scalding. The plants might enjoy all that sun but it isn't good for the fruit. Too much sun will burn their skin. Tomatoes should be shaded from direct sun and this is why over-pruning your plants is not a good idea. The leaves provide much needed shade for the fruit. If the tomatoes overheat they will shrivel and burn. It only has to happen once to ruin the fruit. Too much sunlight exposure can also result in green shoulders. In this case, parts of the tomato never fully ripen, no matter how long they are left out. You can still eat them though. Just cut away the green parts.

---

[*] The Effect of Extreme Temperatures on the Tomato and Pepper Crop. Ontario Ministry of Agricultural, Food and Rural Affairs.

http://www.omafra.gov.on.ca/english/crops/facts/info_tomtemp.htm

Watermelons

Growing melons in containers is not a simple task but it can be done. I had really low expectations the first time I grew watermelons but in the end I was quite pleased with what I was able to grow. For best results with watermelon growing in containers, you need to select an icebox or midget variety such as Sugar Baby, Golden Midget, Early Moonbeam or Cream of Saskatchewan. They produce manageable vines with early melons under 10 lbs in weight.

Getting Started

I have seen them available as starter plants at garden centers along with other melons and squash, but not in great numbers and certainly not the varieties I look for. I have never had problems starting melons from seed in my kitchen window. I usually start them in 3 inch plastic pots. If the soil temperature is above 68°F (20°C), the seeds will happily germinate and it takes about a week for the seedlings to break through the soil surface. The new plants will be ready to go outside after another month, once they have 3 or 4 true leaves on them.

As with other plants started indoors, keep the roots moist and apply a mild fertilizer after the plant has put out its first set of true leaves. Melon plants are said to not transplant very well although I have never had problems with mine. To avoid upsetting them during transplant, don't let them become root bound. If started in a biodegradable container you can transplant the plant and its starter container into its permanent home without having to remove the plant from the starter container. This reduces the risk of disturbing the roots.

It's hard to get an early start with watermelons because they are so sensitive to the cold. For best results, keep the plants inside until the temperatures get up above 68°F (20°C) and give them a week outside to acclimatize before transplanting. I've planted watermelons out early when it was too cool outside for them, but I did that knowing I could bring them inside when the weather turned foul. If you cannot do this, consider having something available to cover them, to protect the young plants from cold winds. Young watermelon plants will quickly wither and fade in cooler temperatures and they are quite intolerant of harsh cold winds.

Growing on the Balcony

You need a big container to grow an icebox variety watermelon plant, but not as big as you might think. Something the size of a storage tote will work nicely. I've grown single, small-size watermelon plants in containers that held no more than 10 gallons of potting soil. The roots will spread and fill a container of this size, but it's nothing compared to the way tomato plants can send out roots. I typically use containers with 12 to 14 inches of soil depth. Provide more if you can.

Use a rich soil mix with a good amount of compost and adequate drainage. It can take a long time to grow a watermelon and their desire for warm temperatures will put limits on the growing season. The optimal growing temperature for watermelons is between 70 and 85°F (20 to 30°C). The more nutrients available for the plant in your potting soil, the quicker the plant will grow.

Large leaves mean heavy transpiration and that places a larger demand on water resources. I've been using self-watering containers for watermelons and they work really well to balance the water load. As for nutrients, just stick to whatever general fertilization routine you have adopted for other plants on the balcony. Nothing special. But as with any large plant grown in a container, keep a close watch for signs of nutrient deficiency and increase fertilizer applications when necessary. I believe a constant flow of nutrients works better for large plants like watermelons grown in containers. A dose of compost or fertilizer added to the container at the start of the season will help as well.

Hand-Pollination

Each watermelon plant will put out male and female flowers and the female flowers will need to be pollinated to produce melons. Unless your balcony is routinely visited by swarms of pollinating insects, you will need to resort to hand-pollination. Female flowers are easy to spot – they have an ovary at the base of the flower that resembles a small watermelon. With luck there will be several male flowers open on your plant when the females are open.

On my watermelon plants I like to aim for two melons per plant. And to get that I will pollinate every female flower that opens. Hand-pollination is only 50% successful so don't hesitate. If you get lucky and manage to start more than two melons, you can remove the weaker of the bunch and let the plant focus its resources on the remaining two.

Supporting Watermelon Vines

It's not practical to let the vines sprawl out all over the floor of the balcony and they won't get much light down there either. If the edge of your balcony is protected by a railing instead of a half wall you could train the vines to grow along that, giving them maximum sunlight exposure. I grow things vertically on my balcony to make the most of the afternoon sunlight, so I use a trellis to grow my watermelons.

A rag being used to hang a melon from its trellis

A melon relaxing in an onion sack hammock

Smaller melon plants grow a few main vines that can easily reach 12 or 13ft (4m) in length with a number of shorter secondary vines. It is a good idea to pinch off some of the secondary vines when you see them forming and let the plant focus its energy on just 2 or 3 vines. Unlike some larger vining plants (like pumpkins), the vines of icebox watermelon plants are fairly easy to weave in and around the openings of a trellis. Melon vines send out tendrils that reach out and grab anything they find and once they take hold of something they maintain a firm grip. The biggest challenge is providing a trellis that won't crash under the weight of the vines and melons. If you know that growing large plants like this is going to be a regular occurrence on your balcony, you should construct a proper trellis structure that you can reuse every season.

When a watermelon does start to form on your vine, don't wait too long to see if the vine and tendrils will be strong enough to support the weight of the melon. Create a sling for it from something like a nylon onion sack, an old T-shirt or stocking. Use material that will not restrict the growth of the melon. Secure the ends of the sling to the trellis to relieve the vines of having to handle the extra weight load.

Harvest

Keep track of when you planted the melon and how long the variety you planted is suppose to take to reach maturity. Time to maturity from transplant for small watermelon varieties is typically between 70 and 100 days. This will help you determine roughly when the melons on your vine should be ready to pick.

I always see people slapping watermelons at the grocery store. Some people appear to know what they are doing but most don't. The purpose is to determine how solid the melon is inside. A hollow melon, one in which the flesh has loosened and is starting to break down, is suppose to sound like a drum. Beating on a melon will send a vibration through the melon to the hand that you are holding the melon with. A dull thud is what you want to feel. This is the sound of a solid melon.

Honestly though, I don't get anything out of pounding on watermelons. When it comes to picking them, there are a few things to watch out for. When ripe, the colour of the skin will start to dull a little and feel rough. If grown on the ground, the spot where the melon was resting on the ground should be yellow and not white but obviously if you grow yours on a trellis you can't rely on this indicator. Something else to look for is the tendril on the vine nearest the melon stem. It will dry out and start to turn brown as the melon ripens. But I've never been able to detect this on my plants. Weight should be another indicator. The melon should feel heavy for its size. If you notice the melon start to shrink a little it is definitely time to pick it. Perhaps even too late. But all of these indicators will only tell you if the melon is ready to pick. You'll have to cut into it to see how it tastes.

Problems

Powdery and downy mildew are common problems I have with melon plants. Spider mites are a problem too. Fortunately, with the plant up on a trellis it is easy to spray a mild solution of soapy water on the undersides of the leaves. On my balcony I like to keep trellised plants out from the wall and closer to the edge of the balcony where they can get more sun. And this lets me get behind them to spray the backs of the leaves and has the added benefit of providing the plant with better circulation.

Malformed immature Sugar Baby watermelon

In an environment buzzing with bees, a female flower will be visited several times by pollen-carrying insects while it is open and receptive. These insects tend to do a thorough job of pollinating which is important; pollen application needs to be consistent across the whole stigma of the female flower otherwise the melon will not mature properly and will develop smaller along one side than the other. This is a typical problem with hand pollinated fruit.

My Favorite Balcony Herbs

Herbs make perfect container plants for the balcony. Some need a good amount of sunlight and heat but in general, they don't mind the wind and most can put up with being neglected. Most herbs take up very little space and you can plant them in any size container you wish. If you like to use herbs in your kitchen, stop buying them from the grocery stores and try growing your own. As with vegetables, stick to the ones you know you'll make use of. Some herbs you can start from seed, but many are best started from cuttings. It's easy to pick up a wide selection of herb starter plants from the garden center in the spring. And this gives you the opportunity to sample the plant (by tasting a leaf) before you buy it. Because with some herbs, not all plants of the same variety taste alike.

Herb	Type	Sunlight	Moisture	Height	Starting from
Basil	Annual	☼	◊◊◊	12" to 24"	Seed or Transplant
Chervil	Annual	◑	◊◊◊	12"	Seed
Chives	Perennial	☼ ◑	◊◊◊	12" to 18"	Seed or Transplant
Coriander	Biennial	☼	◊◊	12" to 24"	Seed
Dill	Annual	☼	◊◊	1' to 4'	Seed
Mint	Perennial	◑	◊◊◊	Up to 24"	Transplant
Oregano	Perennial	☼	◊	12" to 24"	Seed or Transplant
Parsley	Biennial	☼ ◑	◊◊	8 to 16"	Seed or Transplant
Rosemary	Perennial	☼ ◑	◊	Up to 5'	Transplant
Thyme	Perennial	☼ ◑	◊	6" to 12"	Seed or Transplant

A collection of herbs growing on my balcony

Basil

The perfect companion for tomatoes. You can find basil plants in the spring at any garden center. Even the discount grocer in my neighbourhood will sometimes sell potted basil plants. Basil is an annual that needs warm weather to thrive. It grows best in full sunlight and enjoys moist, rich soil. In a container, basil plants can easily grow to between 12 and 24 inches in height. Basil is easy to start from seed and transplants well. I always start my basil from seed indoors in the spring. I grow more basil than any other herb.

In cool weather basil fades fast and stops growing so don't start your basil too early. You can't get a jump on the season with basil if you seed or transplant it too early. I've transplanted it outside early and watched the tiny leaves shrivel and fade away in cool bitter spring winds. Best to wait until the weather warms up a bit. Lately I've been putting my basil seedlings out after the tomatoes, a couple of weeks after my last frost date.

Basil is best used fresh from the plant. The leaves have a tendency to turn brown when stored in the refrigerator. If you grow several plants you can pull a few leaves off of each when you need it and leave the plants to recover and produce more leaves for another day. But the plants will only last so long, eventually flowering and going to seed. Like most herbs, once it flowers it might not taste the same although I've never noticed much of a difference myself. Pinch the growing tips to discourage flowering and force branching which will yield more leaves.

Basil seeds and Sweet Basil leaves

There are several varieties of basil to choose from. Genovese and Sweet Basil are the two I've grown the most. I've grown purple basil just because I thought it looked interesting. I don't think we actually ate any of it though. If you're looking for something different, consider one of the small bush varieties that grow into compact bushy plants with lots of tiny leaves.

Chervil

Chervil is an annual that looks a little like flat leaf parsley or coriander but has a taste closer to that of fennel. Unlike most herbs, chervil really doesn't do well in the heat and goes to seed quickly. Keep its soil moist. It is a rather delicate plant and that's probably why it doesn't show up for sale in garden centers or grocery stores. Thanks to a fussy tap root it does not transplant well either so it's best started from seed in the container in which you intend to grow it. I've found it rather difficult to start.

Chervil seeds and leaves

Once established, chervil, like most other herbs, makes a great container plant. On the balcony it will grow into a compact bushy plant about 12 inches tall. Being in a container means you can move it around to shady spots out of the wind and hot summer sun. Pinch the growing tips to discourage bolting. It works well in salads and as a final garnish in soups. The young tender leaves are the most flavorful. Don't hesitate to harvest and use them before they fade away.

Chives

Chives are easy to grow. Onion chives, the type I grow, are a member of the onion family and form tiny bulbs with long hollow tubular leaves that can reach over 12 inches in height. Another type of chive is the garlic chive which grows tall flat leaves that have a mild garlic taste.

Chives can be grown in full sun or partial shade and do well with a good drink of water from time to time. They are a perennial and can over-winter in a garden, but in a container they might have a harder time surviving. No matter though. Just bring them inside. I've planted chives from seed in small containers and kept them as annuals. They are easy to grow from seed and also very easy to come by at garden centers.

Growing from a bulb, chives have the ability to reproduce asexually. The chive bulbs will split forming two identical bulbs. And then those eventually split, and so on and so on. Over time the chives will grow dense and fill their container. You can pull up the entire clump and separate it into small clumps, repotting each into a new container. The chives will appreciate their newly acquired growing space; this form of propagation is known as division.

Onion chive seeds and flowers

To harvest chives, just cut the leaves an inch or two from the soil surface. Eventually the plant will grow new leaves. Once chives decide to flower they will send up a long flower stalk with a purple flower at the top. Garlic chives form white flowers. Once successfully pollinated, the flower will start to form seeds. The flower stalks are tough and not worth eating but I hear the flowers are quite edible.

Coriander

Although it has a Mediterranean origin, coriander is used in kitchens all around the world. The plant is referred to as coriander and this name is also used for the seeds of the plant. But the leaves are typically known as cilantro. Chinese parsley is another name used for the leaves. All parts of the plant have uses. Ground-up seeds are a popular South Asian spice. The

leaves are used to enhance the flavor of dishes across Asia and Latin America. Even the roots find uses in soups and teas. Coriander is prized for it's medicinal qualities and is said to be an aphrodisiac.

The seeds have a slightly citrus flavor with just a hint of the same flavor that is found in the leaves. And the leaves have a taste that is described as everything from soapy to rancid. Some people have an aversion to the taste of the leaves but that doesn't seem to be the case in my home.

In containers on the balcony, the plants will likely peak at 12 inches in height. In the right climate it can be grown as a biennial but for most northern gardeners, it's an annual. Although related to parsley, it presents different growing challenges. It can be somewhat difficult to start from seed. I have started it early indoors from seed and transplanted it but it took a while for the little transplants to bounce back from the shock. It has a fussy tap root that does not like to be transplanted so just seed it in the container you wish to grow it.

It can be somewhat temperamental, going to seed quickly and fading fast. For this reason I don't see a need to start it early. I have not been able to grow coriander plants to the size or vigor of parsley and I would describe the plants I have grown as weak and scraggly when compared to my parsley. But I understand that it does have the ability to grow into a lush bushy plant if the conditions are right. It will likely do better with less moisture and a fast draining soil. One recommended method for growing it is in small succession plantings, staggered every week or so. Use it on a cut-and-come-again basis. Don't fight it and just let it go to seed and wither when it wants to.

The leaves of the plant do not store well. Do not store damp leaves in the refrigerator and only wash them when you are ready to use them. A bouquet of coriander will only keep for a few days in the refrigerator. It's better to use the leaves fresh from the plant. After all, that's the whole point of growing it yourself.

Coriander seeds and flowers

Dill

Dill is a simple plant to grow and does well in containers on the balcony. The seeds germinate quickly and the plants grow fast. There is no need to transplant dill seedlings. Just plant it in the container in which you plan to grow it. Dill grows a deep tap root that does not like being disturbed so don't bother with transplants although I've transplanted it many times without much trouble. Grow it in a deep container to let the roots grow deep and you will be rewarded with a large dill plant.

In a container on the balcony, grow dill as an annual. In warmer climates it can be grown as a perennial. Dill can grow up to three feet tall. I generally find that the taller it grows, the more spaced out its leaves get. Taller plants don't necessarily mean more leaves. It is a slender plant and will appreciate a bit of extra support to keep it upright on windy days. It prefers sunny conditions and moist, well-drained soil. And I hear it is a poor companion plant for tomatoes, but great for cucumbers.

In some cultures, the seeds are prized. But in others, it's the leaves that are desired. Dill plants will eventually form a wide flower head and when that happens, all leaf production on the plant will stop. You might be able to cut the entire plant down at this point and have it grow again to give you a second harvest. But I've never tried this myself. Dill leaves work well with butter and cream cheese. Mix it with baked buttered baby potatoes or fresh buttered peas. I like stuffing huge amounts of it into the cavity of a fish for baking.

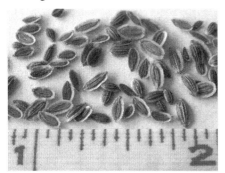 

Dill seeds and flowers

Mint

Mint thrives in containers and is easily propagated. It is an incredibly forgiving plant that does well in partial shade and can tolerate some abuse. Being a perennial, you can bring it indoors to over-winter. Some varieties are hardy to zone 3 and with the right protection from the cold, just might be able to survive a winter on your balcony. There are several different varieties of mint. I've grown English Mint, Apple Mint and Spearmint purchased from garden centers. Few mint plants will grow true from seed because many of them are hybrids. This means that a new plant grown from seed will not be identical to its parent. You're best to purchase plants (or find cuttings) instead.

Mint spreads by sending out runners. These can form above or below the soil surface. As the runners grow, they form nodes from which roots and new shots form. Each of these nodes is the beginning of another mint plant. The invasive nature of mint is legendary and the best way to keep it from spreading out of control is to grow it in a container. But avoid planting it in a container with other plants as it will quickly spread, crowding out its neighbours and dominating the container.

To propagate your mint plants you can look for new plants popping up near the original plant. These will be growing off a runner under the soil. You should be able to separate this new plant from the main one and replant it in another container. It is also easy to grow new plants from cuttings. Just remove a fresh branch from the donor plant, remove the leaves from the lower half of the branch and insert it into a container of moist soil. Eventually the cutting should form new roots and grow into a new plant.

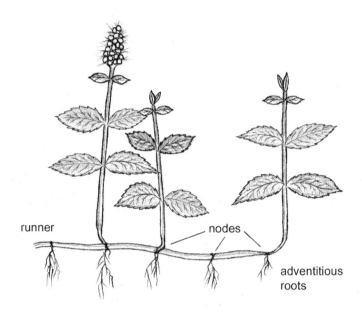

Below ground mint runner

Above ground mint runner trying to find a new home

Oregano

Oregano is a perennial Mediterranean herb. There are several oregano varieties, all with slightly different tastes. A common oregano cultivar is Greek oregano. But even within a group of plants bearing that name, there will be a wide discrepancy in flavor and growing habits.

I've grown Greek oregano started from seed. However the seeds are extremely small so starting it in this manner can be somewhat tedious. A better way to grow Oregano is to sample the plants at the garden center and select one with an agreeable taste. But even if you select a tasty seedling to start with, keep in mind that as the plant matures, its taste will likely change also.

The oregano I've grown starts off slow but spreads into a dense mat that reaches out over its container. In small containers, it never reaches much more than a foot in height. Although it enjoys full sun, partially sunny conditions will work also. It doesn't like its soil being overly moist but I've found that it sometimes gets a little thirsty, particularly in hot dry weather. Hot arid conditions will quickly suck moisture from the delicate leaves, causing them to wilt in the summer heat. On the other hand, oregano doesn't appreciate sitting around in overly moist soil either. Good drainage and frequent watering during hot weather will keep it happy. Oregano plants are not heavy feeders and do not need nutrient-rich soil to thrive.

A small container of Greek oregano

Pinch the growing branch tips to encourage branching and prevent flowering. And don't be afraid to abuse it a little. Let it experience an occasional drought to bring out its flavor. As with most herbs, the common wisdom is to use the leaves before the plant flowers, because the intensity of its flavor will diminish rapidly once the plant starts to flower. Being a perennial, you can move it to a sunny indoor location in the winter.

Oregano is very easy to dry and dried oregano maintains its flavor. I actually prefer the taste of dried oregano over fresh. The fresh oregano I've grown always tastes a little too sharp and acidic for my liking. Oregano is great with tomato dishes and is a 'must use' herb in any tomato-based sauce. But when given the choice, I prefer to use fresh thyme instead.

Parsley

Flat leaf parsley is what I like to grow instead of the curly leaf parsley most commonly used as a decoration on your dinner plate. I like to add fresh chopped parsley to salads and it is particularly nice in a bean salad. It's easy to grow in containers but can be a little difficult to get started.

You can purchase plants from a garden center but parsley also starts from seed and that's how I grow mine. Apparently parsley seeds can take 3 or 4 weeks to germinate but mine never seem to take more than two weeks. Like all seeds, parsley seeds are coated with a natural inhibitor that prevents germination. But in the case of parsley seed, this inhibitor is particularly stubborn. Soaking the seed for a few hours before planting will speed up the breakdown of the inhibitor and make the seeds germinate faster. Starting them indoors at room temperature also helps speed up the germination process. It tends to get quite leggy when grown indoors from seed on a window sill but that doesn't seem to bother parsley too much. When I transplant it I just bury it up to its crown and it does just fine.

I grow my parsley in partially sunny conditions. Unlike some herbs, it appreciates a nutrient-rich soil and I find it to be a rather thirsty plant that enjoys daily watering. Two or three plants are all you need for casual use. I pick branches and leaves off as needed, but by the end of the season I usually still have more than I need. Parsley is a biennial, meaning it will go to seed in its second year of growth before dying. On my balcony it is grown as an annual.

Cut the old growth to encourage new growth. Keeping the plant pruned will give you a much larger and healthier plant over time. I once cut a good size plant down to the ground at the end of a season and left it for dead. But within a couple of weeks it was up and growing again and it continued to do so with minimal attention until it was put down again for good by a frost. I was quite surprised at how resilient it was. Cutting the plant back seemed to give it new life.

Parsley seeds and a flat leaf parsley leaf

Rosemary

Rosemary is an evergreen frost-tender perennial that makes a great balcony container plant. It can handle a bit of neglect and will even survive brief periods of drought. There are many different cultivars of rosemary with different flavors and growing habits. Some grow as small compact container plants and others into tall 4 or 5 foot bushes. Rosemary will occasionally flower, with small delicate flowers of white, blue or violet depending on the variety.

Don't bother trying to grow rosemary from seed. Pick up some small plants from a garden center instead. Mediterranean in origin, rosemary is used to growing in hot, sunny and humid conditions. Being frost-tender means even the slightest exposure to frost will kill it. Rosemary is hardy to zone 8 but doesn't mind coming indoors to over-winter in a sunny window sill until spring. It will not appreciate the dry winter air indoors so you may have to mist it down occasionally. Although it appreciates dry soil, it will be happier in a humid growing environment. Rosemary grows best in full sun but I've found it can manage quite well in the partial sunlight conditions of my balcony.

The last rosemary plant I purchased spent a few winters in the kitchen window before it got too unmanageable. It was quite potent and all you had to do was brush up against it to release a wave of rosemary aroma. Regularly prune rosemary to promote tender new growth. And when the stems get long, pinch the ends to force branching. Occasionally repot it, perhaps each spring, to give the roots more growing space and get some fresh nutrients into the soil. Container grown rosemary will start to look un-kept and wild after a few years. The lower stems will be woody and without leaves. This might be a good time to start over.

Rosemary propagates easily. Just clip off a healthy looking fresh stem that is a few inches long. Remove the leaves from the lower inch or two of the stem and stick it in a small container of potting soil. Keep it moist and in no time, new roots will develop. Be patient with newly started rosemary plants. It can take a while for them to grow to a good size for harvesting.

A rosemary cutting after a few weeks of being planted and a rosemary flower

Rosemary works well with roasted meats such as lamb and pork. You might find it on some Mediterranean breads. Focaccia bread comes to mind. It is also a popular choice for flavoring olive oil. But even if you don't want to eat it, a container of rosemary will still make a great addition to your balcony garden.

Thyme

I think thyme is the perfect herb for container growing. It's a small and compact plant that doesn't require much attention and is really big on flavor and aroma. It has too many uses in the kitchen to mention. My favorite use for it is in tomato sauces. Its tiny leaves pack so much flavor that you don't need very much. In some dishes you don't even need to strip the leaves. Just toss in an entire sprig and pull it out before eating. Thyme also retains most of its flavor after being dried.

The most common variety of thyme is *Thymus vulgaris* or simply common thyme. Other forms of common thyme you may encounter are garden thyme, French thyme, German thyme or English thyme. They are all pretty much the same.

Thyme is an evergreen perennial, hardy down to zone 5 and perhaps lower. Being such a small plant, it's better just to bring container grown thyme indoors in the winter, instead of hoping it survives outside. There are several different varieties that all grow into compact plants no more than 12 inches in height. It doesn't require much moisture and potting soil that drains readily will be appreciated. Thyme enjoys lots of sunlight but can manage in partial sunlight as well.

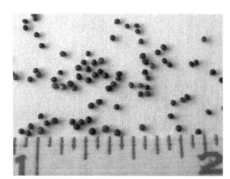

Thyme seeds and a cutting ready for transplant

It is easy to find thyme in the garden centers and the best way to start thyme is with a starter plant: something you can taste and sniff before committing yourself to a particular variety. You can start it from seed but the seeds are very tiny and a pain to deal with. And there is no guarantee that what you grow from seed will taste all that great. I've grown German thyme from seed and it turned out alright. But it's much easier to purchase plants. I've also grown lemon thyme which has variegated leaves and a hint of citrus flavor.

After a few years of growth, like rosemary, thyme will start looking a little ragged and unmanageable. By then you will have had lots of time to propagate it which is easy to do. A single stem with the leaves removed from the lower inch or two and inserted into some moist potting soil will take root after a few weeks. The growing habits of this little bushy plant also make it easy to propagate by layering.

Layering is a method of propagation where a long stem is trained to grow along the surface of the soil in another container placed next to the donor plant. Where the stem touches the soil surface in the new container, strip off the leaves and lightly bury it. It can be held in place with a small loop of bent wire. In time, the stem will send new roots into the new container. It can then be cut free of the donor plant, providing you with a new plant to grow.

Layering works great for propagating herbs such as Thyme and Rosemary

Common Problems and Pests

I find the Internet to be an incredible resource when it comes to solving problems with plants. Just enter a few keywords describing the symptoms into a search engine and a whole host of possible causes and solutions appear, with images. Similarly, posting a simple question to a good gardening forum will usually lead to immediate assistance. Especially if you can post an image of the troubled plant.

Aphids

I'll never forget my first encounter with aphids on the balcony. They hitched a ride up here on some starter pepper plants from a garden center and for years after that I had problems with them. Aphids are small insects that cling to the underside of plant leaves and thrive in and around open and un-open flower buds. They suck juices from the plant causing it much stress and can carry and transmit plant viruses. Plants with extreme aphid infestations don't grow much and have a hard time setting fruit.

A mother aphid and her offspring

There are several different species of aphid and they don't all fancy the same types of plant. Some plants they like and some they don't. For example, I never have a problem with aphids on tomatoes, but on my balcony they seem to love peppers (hot or sweet, makes no difference).

The problem with aphids is that they multiply at an astonishing rate. The females reproduce asexually by a process known as parthenogenesis. They do not need males to reproduce and for most of the season all they produce are female offspring. They live between 20 and 40 days and can produce something like 5 offspring each day from the time they are a week old.

Aphids excrete a sweet liquid when they feed known as honeydew. It's easy to spot - just look for shiny wet patches on the tops of lower leaves and chances are there will be an aphid colony on one of the leaves above it. Some insects feed on this honeydew. Wasps become a problem on my balcony when there are lots of aphids around as the wasps like to eat the sweet honeydew. Some ant species that eat honeydew go so far as to herd aphids colonies to protect them from predatory insects.

At some point during the growing season, some aphid species will start producing winged females who fly off to seek plants on which to start new colonies. And in the fall, some aphid colonies start producing male aphids and these mate with the females so they can produce aphid eggs that will survive the winter and hatch new aphids in the spring.

Aphids have a number of natural predators, including ladybug and lacewing larvae. Neither of these show up on my balcony very often, but sometimes I notice quite a few hoverfly larvae hunting for aphids on my plants. The aphid colonies on these plants disappear almost overnight. But after the hoverfly larvae turn into adults and leave the plants, the aphids eventually return.

That's the problem with growing plants in a semi-enclosed environment. Without natural predators to keep them in check, pests like aphids thrive. I've used sprays of soapy water and neem oil without much luck. Apparently the neem oil takes a while to work on the aphids, affecting them by making it impossible for them to feed. And maybe at some level it does work, but with a huge thriving colony of aphids all it likely does is slow them down for a while.

Using a spray bottle to blast them off the undersides of the leaves is effective. You'll immediately see them regrouping on the soil surface before marching back up the stems again but it does give your plant a good break from the attack. I've heard that placing shiny foil paper below uninfested plants will distract the flying aphids and keep them from landing on the nearby plants to start a new colony.

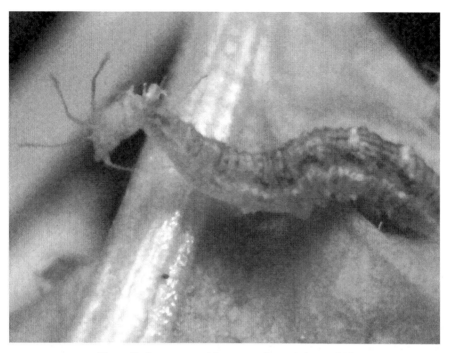

Hoverfly larvae snacking on a plump juicy aphid

As soon as you spot aphids on any plant, remove the aphids (squish them) and isolate the plant if you can. If it's just one new plant out of several, then you might want to consider getting rid of the plant to save yourself from trouble later.

Whiteflies

If you give one of your plants a good shake and a cloud of small white moth-like flies rise up from it, you have a whitefly infestation. These tiny flies, which are actually related to aphids, are less than a few millimeters in length and attack plants in a similar way to aphids and spider mites. The two most common varieties of whitefly are greenhouse and silverleaf. They vary a bit in size and appearance, and in the plants they prefer, but they all enjoy doing the same thing: sucking the juices from the underside of leaves and laying a huge number of eggs.

The leaves they feed from eventually yellow and wilt, causing much plant stress. Equally as damaging are the plant diseases they can spread. And to round out the threat, they secrete honeydew as they feed, which coats the lower leaves on the plant leading to possible mold and mildew issues.

Whitefly eggs, which are impossible to see with the naked eye, are laid out on the underside of a leaf in a circular pattern and are covered with a white film. There are a few stages of development between egg and adult which can take as little as 6 weeks to complete depending on temperatures and species. During the early stages of development the larvae and pupa remain on the leaves and feed. Once they reach adulthood, females start laying eggs right away and can lay a few hundred eggs over the course of their lifetime. The pre-adult whiteflies are usually found on young tender leaves whereas the adults tend to gather on older growth.

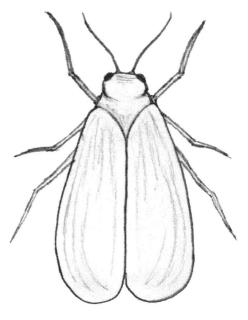

Whiteflies do have natural predators: to name a few, ladybugs, lacewing larvae, and tiny parasitic wasps that feed exclusively on whitefly larvae. But you likely won't be seeing many of these on your balcony. Your best option for controlling whitefly colonies is to spray the plant with a diluted solution of soapy water. The adults are attracted to the colour yellow (so I hear) and sticky yellow traps placed near an infested plant may trap a few. Apparently marigolds will repel them as will nasturtiums. And I've also heard claims that you can use a vacuum cleaner to suck up the adults. Just give the plant a shake and collect them in flight.

Whitefly problems usually start with plants brought home from a garden center. I've only seen them a couple of times and they've never caused my plants much noticeable damage. Whiteflies thrive in greenhouse environments and cannot survive a good frost. And for those of us living in the North, that is the best way to get rid of them: wait for winter and sleep well knowing they won't be back in the spring.

Spider Mites

Spider Mites are tiny mites that generate a fine webbing to protect their colony from predators, hence the name spider mite. One of the most common is the two spotted spider mite, identified by the two large spots on each side of its body. They are nearly microscopic in size, generally under 0.5 mm in length, and thus very difficult to see. The damage they create and their webbing is usually what you will notice first.

They cling to the underside of the leaves and suck juices from plant cells at an alarming rate. The damage this creates starts as a light yellow stippling of the leaf that eventually spreads to the entire leaf, turning it yellow or brown and making it very brittle. If left to thrive they quickly take over the entire plant, killing every leaf and leaving the plant for dead. Being so small, they can easily be blown by the wind from plant to plant.

Leaf damage caused by spider mites

They thrive in warm dry weather; at around 80°F (27°C) eggs hatch in as little as 3 days and the baby mites can reach adulthood in as little as 5 days. They only live for a couple of weeks but females can lay hundreds of eggs in that time meaning they spread fast! Once you notice the damage it won't be long before they completely take over. Female spider mites can over-winter on dead plant matter or in the surface layer of your potting soil so expect them to be back in the spring.

They do have quite a few natural predators that will likely never find their way onto your balcony. Apparently lacewing larvae love eating them. On the balcony, a diluted solution of ordinary dish soap applied to the underside of infected plant leaves will be your best defense. Avoid an overly concentrated spay as this can burn the plant leaves and cause just as much damage to the plant as the mites themselves. It may take a bit of trial and error to get the right dilution and different soap brands will have a different potency. I add a little neem oil to mine and I find it kills them almost instantly. But this does not affect the eggs so future applications will be necessary to keep the colony from spreading.

Despite the damage they create and their persistence, I don't mind the spider mite infestations as much as the aphids because I know I can control the spider mites. I just keep a spray bottle handy, topped up with a soapy solution. It only takes a few minutes to mist down the few plants they infest. On my balcony their favorite plants seem to be melons, cucumbers, beans and peas.

Mildew

There are two forms of mildew you need to worry about on your balcony: downy mildew and powdery mildew. Cucumbers and pumpkins are two plants that always suffer from downy mildew on my balcony. I've also seen it on my peas and fava beans. And at the end of the season, my tomatoes sometime show dustings of powdery mildew.

Downey mildew shows up as blocky yellow spots on the tops of leaves. On the underside of the leaves, beneath the spots, will be a grey powdery growth. Eventually the spots turn brown as the affected leaf tissue dies. The mildew eventually spreads to the entire leaf, killing it and thereby reducing the amount of sunlight the plant can absorb for photosynthesis. The end result is stunted growth and lower fruit yield.

Powdery mildew is a white powdery fungus that appears on the top surface of a plant's leaves. It is not as lethal as downy mildew, but it does spread and will cover the leaf, blocking its ability to absorb sunlight and photosynthesize.

Both forms of plant mildew thrive in similar conditions. They love moisture and humidity. The spores can be transported every way imaginable: on the wind, in the water, in the soil, on the seeds... Crowding your plants will cause mildew to flourish. Too much shade keeps temperatures low, which will encourage mildew growth. Avoid watering the leaves of your plants or leaving them wet. Again, too much moisture means higher humidity and more mildew.

There are hybrid plant varieties available that are bred to be resistant to mildew. If you are starting from seed and have a choice between one that is resistant and one that isn't, consider taking the resistant variety. Treat infected areas of the plant immediately, particularly in the case of downy mildew, or remove infected leaves entirely. All it takes is a slight breeze to spread the spores to other leaves and plants resulting in further infection. Infected growth should be disposed of. Try not to mix the infected leaf matter back into your soil or composter. The mold spores can fester there and strike again when conditions are right.

You can purchase anti-fungal sprays that will quickly take out the mildew. As usual, a light misting of a mild detergent solution will also do the trick. Neem oil will keep the mildew under control too. Don't forget to spray the undersides of the leaves. Once you see it on a plant and apply a treatment, keep a close watch over the plant. The mildew will most likely return. Leaf tissue affected by downy mildew will not recover so do not let it spread for too long.

Nutrient Deficiencies

Before concluding that your plants are suffering from a nutrient deficiency be sure to rule out some other likely causes. Over or under-watering can cause leaves to curl and drop just like some nutrient deficiencies. Also look for insects on the underside of the leaves feeding on plant juices. If more than one deficiency is present, the symptoms may not be easily interpreted.

Also consider soil pH. If the pH of your potting soil is too far outside the typical range of 6.0 to 7.0, your plants will have a harder time getting the nutrients they need. A new potting soil fresh out of the bag will likely have its pH properly adjusted for growing plants. But over time, as potting soil materials break down, the pH buffering ability of the potting soil will fade. The addition of mineral salts found in inorganic fertilizers and tap water will also result in pH shifts. Which way the pH drifts depends on a number of factors. If the salts are not flushed from the soil or reduced by some other means, the buildup will not only affect the pH of the potting soil, but will also inhibit the ability of the plant's roots to take in moisture and nutrients.

If you've started with a good amount of organic matter in your potting soil, you should not have any issues with micronutrients. And if you suspect there is a problem with micronutrient deficiency in one or more of your container plants, apply a good liquid organic fertilizer derived from kelp or seaweed. These contain a whole host of macro and micro nutrients and lots of other good things. Notice how the organic fertilizers always seem to have everything you need?

Nutrient deficiency causing Interveinal Chlorosis (yellowing between the veins)

Dark spots common on plants suffering from a nutrient deficiency

Symptoms of Macronutrient Deficiencies

Nitrogen (N)	Leaves turn yellow starting with those lower on the plant. Overall growth will be hindered.
Phosphorous (P)	Older plant leaves will develop a purple tinge. Tips of the leaves will dry out and look burned. The plant will have a hard time setting fruit.
Potassium (K)	Leaves develop a burnt appearance around the edges. Leaves start to yellow around the leaf veins.
Magnesium (Mg)	Edges of the leaves turn yellow and new leaves may be yellow with dark spots.
Calcium (Ca)	Common in tomatoes. Fruit forms with a black moldy patch known as blossom end rot.
Sulfur (S)	Leaves turn yellow starting with the new leaves. Growth is hindered.

Symptoms of Micronutrient Deficiencies

Boron (B)	New growth dies off and growth is inhibited.
Copper (Cu)	Growth hindered as leaves turn dark green, curl and eventually drop.
Iron (Fe)	Leaves yellow between their veins.
Manganese (Mn)	Slow growth with yellowing leaves and dead spots.
Molybdenum (Mo)	Old leaves turn yellow and new growth is light green.
Zinc (Zn)	Growth is slow and new growth stunted. Yellowing of the leaves between the veins.

Source: Guide to Symptoms of Plant Nutrient Deficiencies issued by Shanyn Hosie and Lucy Bradle, The University of Arizona Cooperative Extension. Publication AZ1106, May 1999

If you follow a regular routine of fertilizer application and have prepared your potting soil properly at the beginning of the season, these problems should not occur. But if they do, the obvious solution is to step up the fertilizer application. Or switch to one that leans more towards providing those missing nutrients. But be warned that over-compensating for an apparent lack of one nutrient can lead to other problems. Over use of inorganic fertilizers can burn a plant's roots, evident by burnt patches on leaves caused by lack of moisture intake by a damaged root system. Also, a nutrient imbalance that results in an excess or lack of some nutrients can actually block a plant's ability to take in others.

For me, nutrient deficiencies come in the spring when I'm starting out and late in the season when the plants are fruiting and have been growing for some time. It doesn't take long for a seedling to deplete the little bit of nutrient it receives from its starter soil. Leaf drop and discoloration are common in new seedlings when they don't get a good dose of nutrients early on. The same thing happens with my older plants. My big tomatoes always start to look battle-hardened by late fall. The lower leaves yellow and curl and some start to develop purple and brown spots. This is usually a sign that whatever compost and dry fertilizer I added to the soil earlier in the season has been exhausted.

Cutworms

Cutworms are moth caterpillars and not really worms at all. They are plump looking, about an inch long, grey or green with light stripes. The moths lay their eggs in your potting soil or under a pile of dead leaves and when the larvae appear, they are hungry. They are known as cutworms because of their feeding habits. Some will attack the stems of new plants and essentially cut the plants down. They are voracious feeders. Some are sensitive to light, living out of sight by day and feeding at night. When threatened they curl up and play dead.

They are not much of a threat to balcony garden. I figured they would never be a problem for me but I do occasionally find them under

A frightened cutworm on the end of my little garden shovel

piles of old leaves. And I do sometimes find plants with damage consistent with cutworm activity, but I have yet to see any committing the crime.

I don't see too many moths up here. My pigeon netting has openings big enough for large insects to enter and leave through if they are persistent enough. I suppose a big moth gets lucky every now and then and manages to get in to find a suitable egg laying site.

Pigeons

Pigeons will not necessarily ruin your crops, but a balcony garden will provide them with several roosting and nesting opportunities. They're not that loud and certainly not aggressive or dangerous, but they are capable of making a tremendous mess of your balcony. Their droppings carry quite a stench even when dry and leave behind a residue that takes a bit of scrubbing to remove. Dust from these dried droppings can carry some nasty fungal diseases too so for the health and welfare of yourself and others it is best to keep your balcony free of their mess.

The pigeons we find in North America that flock around buildings in urban centers were introduced as pets from Europe. Thanks to their cliff-dwelling ancestry, they quickly adapted to urban living. Although their primary diet is grain, urban pigeons have no trouble obtaining food from the trash or a hand-out in the park. Although they are scavengers, they are also communal birds that flock together and mate for life.

I've seen a number of tricks to help keep them away from balconies. Some people tie plastic bags to their railings, with the idea being that the wind will rustle the bags and scare the pigeons away. You can purchase life-like plastic owls to perch on your railings. Some even have self-bobbing heads, but they are rather costly. I used to find that just constantly shooing them away and banging on the windows would be enough to make them feel uncomfortable and want to roost elsewhere. And for the most part, that will work. Until a pair comes around ready to start a family.

They breed during all months of the year laying one or two eggs per clutch. They are not very fussy about where they nest and will use whatever they can find on your balcony for nesting material. I found a pair attempting to nest on my balcony once using a few chop sticks arranged in a circle as a nest! Once they settle on a nesting area they'll keep coming back to it since egg-laying usually comes shortly after. They don't have much choice so even if you scare them off a number of times, they always seem to come back. You really need to remove all nesting materials from the area and close off all hiding spaces they may find suitable for nesting. Boxes, lumber, garbage, plant containers… all create perfect little private nesting locations.

The best way to keep pigeons off your balcony is with netting made from a light plastic mesh that will not rot or tear or obstruct your view too much. The net must be anchored to the building securely leaving no openings of any kind around the outside edges. I had netting professionally installed over my balcony and haven't

All openings covered with netting

been bothered by pigeons since. Sadly though it does take away from the view. You always notice the net when you're out there, but I think it's a small price to pay. For safety and aesthetic reasons, consider having it done professionally and make sure you have permission from your building manager or landlord to have it installed.

Moving Beyond the Balcony

What if you don't have enough space on your balcony to do what you want? What if you outgrow your space and want to do more? Or perhaps conditions just aren't right on your balcony to grow everything you want. Then what? Here are a few things I would consider doing if and when I get to the point where I need to leave the balcony.

Take It Indoors

There are advantages to growing indoors. You have control over the environment: temperature, light, heat and air movement. But there are also disadvantages and providing the right environment can be costly.

A lot of buildings are now being built with sunrooms instead of balconies. However even with all that sunlight streaming through the windows, you may still need to resort to supplemental lighting. Without a sunroom you can still keep small potted plants alive indoors under growlights. And baby greens can grow to a size suitable for harvesting even if you don't have the space or money for a large lighting setup. There are a lot of expensive growing systems available that have adjustable height lighting strips under which you can grow a number of short leafy plants. But to grow large plants you need some serious lighting and lots of space.

An ideal way to grow indoors if you have the space and like to experiment and tinker with stuff is hydroponics. Growing in this manner involves no soil. All nutrients are provided in a solution that the plant's roots grow into.

In a properly functioning hydroponic system the plants get all the water they need. There is no need to worry about under or over-watering. The hydroponics solution can be re-circulated and aerated to provide adequate oxygen to the roots. All nutrients are strictly controlled. The ability to control the growing environment with precision means you can consistently get a decent crop. Bad weather is not an issue. But it's not all good. Mistakes are costly. Hydroponic systems can also be expensive and require a lot of attention.

Ebb and flow hydroponic systems, also referred to as flood and drain, are the most popular, are easy to set up and don't require much maintenance. These systems work by routinely pumping a nutrient-rich hydroponics solution into a bed where the plants are held. It then drains back into a reservoir where it is aerated until the next pumping cycle. Search the Internet and you should be able to find several simple plans for constructing your own inexpensive system.

Another development in the hydroponics world is the window garden. Plants are grown in plastic bottles suspended in a sunny window and fed with hydroponic solutions. What's really interesting about this is the community that has sprung up around the idea. It is like a cross between a community garden and an open source software project. Information and do-it-yourself plans are available at http://www.windowfarms.org.

Find Some Free Space

If you're up to the challenge, you could take to the streets and start planting in just about any neglected patch of space you can find. Gardening in this manner is known as guerrilla gardening and it generally means planting in spaces you don't have permission to plant in. Some of your gardening activities may have to be done under cover of night to avoid drawing too much attention. And for those hard to reach fenced off spaces, consider seed bombs. You can learn about this and several other urban guerilla gardening tactics at http://www.guerrillagardening.org

But if you don't want to break any laws and just want a quiet place to grow some crops, consider cultivating the yards of your family, friends and neighbours. You don't need to plan out a garden for them, just plant a few containers and place them in their backyards. You might even be able to convince them to water them for you but don't forget to share the harvest.

My building occupies a fairly large piece of property; I'm certain that if enough owners got together and presented a decent plan to the other owners and the board of directors, we could dedicate some of the property to vegetable gardening space. Not every condo board, property management company or landlord is going to be sympathetic to your cause but then again, anything is possible. You may meet like-minded neighbours who like the idea of a gardening space right in their backyard. Community gardens do require lots of effort from willing volunteers to maintain and manage the site. But there's really not much to lose. If it doesn't work out, re-seed the area with grass and be done with it.

Community Gardening

Community gardens are plots of land managed by volunteers who work the land collectively. The land might be donated private land or public land. I've seen them under power lines, along railway tracks, behind churches, in laneways and in abandoned yards. Generally, they end up in spaces that wouldn't otherwise be used. But unlike the guerrilla gardeners, the community gardeners have permission to plant gardens in these spaces.

Some are set up specifically to beautify neglected urban areas whereas others allow those of us without the space an opportunity to grow our own food. Some are group gardens maintained by a network of volunteers and others consist of plots loaned out to individuals. One thing they all have in common is cooperation: a coming together of people with a common interest, helping one another to achieve goals and have a good time.

If you're looking for a little plot of land for your own gardening purposes, expect to have to pay dues or volunteer for general upkeep of the garden. Some may have restrictions on what you can grow. Also, expect a waiting list. Community gardens are popular in some cities, particularly where space is limited. Individual plot sizes will vary but the spaces provided are generally equivalent to good size kitchen gardens. In Europe, similar community garden plots are much bigger and usually referred to as allotments. In some countries, the land is leased and the allotments are large enough to justify outbuildings for tool storage or a little cottage.

A simple Internet search for "community garden" with the name of your city should point you to the community garden networks in your area and they should be able to provide all the information and advice you need. The Toronto Community Garden Network at http://www.tcgn.ca is a perfect example of what to look for.

Index

Made in the USA
Columbia, SC
24 March 2021